North to the Orient

Anne Morrow Lindbergh

NORTH TO THE
ORIENT

A Harvest/HBJ Book
Harcourt Brace Jovanovich, Publishers
New York and London

Requests for permission to make copies of
any part of the work should be mailed to:
Permissions, Harcourt Brace Jovanovich, Publishers,
757 Third Avenue, New York, N.Y. 10017

Printed in the United States of America

Library of Congress Number 35-27279

ISBN 0-15-667140-9

B C D E F G H I J

Contents

Preface

A Preface is perhaps more for the writer than for the reader. There comes a moment when the things one has written, even a traveler's memories, stand up and demand a justification. They require an explanation. They query, "Who am I? What is my name? Why am I here?" They block the road and will not be put off. One must sit down quietly and reply to their questions in a preface.

This introduction seems unusually necessary in my case, because the anomalous collection of chapters before me, purporting to be an account of an air voyage, evades classification, will not fit the conventional standards and measurements, but stands, nameless, awkward and shy, asking to be introduced.

It is perhaps easier to introduce it negatively, to say what it is not, to clear away the underbrush of illusions, so that neither writer nor reader be disappointed in what follows.

I have not written a technical account of a survey flight on the great circle route from New York to Tokyo. I do not know enough to write one, and if I did, the time for doing so would be past. Aviation moves a long way in four years. No geographical knowledge can be gained from reading my story. We constructed no maps or charts, and I have not even kept a scientific record of all the territory passed. It is not in any sense a guidebook. Our stops were so short and hurried that only a superficial picture remains. Nor is each point on our route portrayed, but only those which seem to warrant description for the vividness of impression.

What, then, is this collection of chapters? How explain it? Why did I write it? There is, of course, always the personal satisfaction of writing down one's own experiences so they may be saved, caught and pinned under glass, hoarded against the winter of forgetfulness. Time has been cheated a little, at least in one's own life, and a personal, trivial immortality of an old self assured. And there is another personal satisfaction: that of the people who like to recount their adventures, the diary-keepers, the story-tellers, the letter-writers, a strange race of people who feel half cheated of an experience unless it is retold. It does not really exist until it is put into words. As though a little doubting or dull, they could not see it until it is repeated. For, paradoxically enough, the more unreal an experience becomes—translated from real action into unreal words, dead symbols for life itself—the more vivid it grows. Not only does it seem more vivid, but its essential core becomes clearer. One says excitedly to an audience, "Do you see—I can't tell you how strange it was—we all of us felt . . ." although actually, at the time of the incident, one was not conscious of such a feeling, and only became so in the retelling. It is as inexplicable as looking all afternoon at a gray stone on a beach, and not realizing, until one tries to put it on canvas, that it is in reality bright blue.

And what is the bright-blue stone of our trip? What essential quality has come out in the telling? It is not in the flying alone, nor in the places alone, nor alone in the time; but in a peculiar blending of all three, which resulted in a quality of magic—a quality that belongs to fairy tales. It was not that we arrived in Baker Lake on August third by plane, but that three hours of flying had brought us from the modern port of Churchill to a place where no white woman had ever been before. It was not only that we flew from Baker Lake to Aklavik in twelve hours, by the midnight sun, but that while flying over those gray wastes south of Victoria Land, isolated and wild as the moon, I could hear through my ear-phones the noisy chatter of big cities over the edge of the world. At northernmost Point Barrow, we flew into an isolated settlement, still waiting for its new year's supply of provisions, and flew out again, independent as the wind, passing their ice-blocked ship, far below us in the sea, on our way to Nome. Over the Chishima Islands in fog, radio told us of weather and harbors ahead. A barefoot fisherman took us into his thatched hut when we landed in bad weather in Kunashiri. The next morning, in clear skies, after a twenty-minute flight, we were in Nemuro and civilization. With nothing but flood beneath us in China, we were within easy distance of food and safety.

It was a magic caused by the collision of modern methods and old ones; modern history and ancient; accessibility and isolation. And it was a magic which could only strike spark about that time. A few years earlier, from the point of view of aircraft alone, it would have been impossible to reach these places; a few years later, and there will be no such isolation.

Perhaps a real magician is only a few steps ahead of his amazed audience, as the Yankee at King Arthur's court, who could prophesy the eclipse. Our modern plane was just a few steps ahead of life at Baker Lake and Barrow and Kunashiri; and therefore it was marvelous to us as well as to them. One has only to see that chasm between accessibility and isolation—narrow, so one could reach across, but deep as time—to appreciate what can bridge it. For though it is easy enough to rub the lamp and have one's wish granted, or to say "Abracadabra" and sail away on a carpet, sometimes the magic fails. The lamp is broken; the word is forgotten; or a spark sets fire to the carpet—and where are you? East of the sun and west of the moon, and you must find the way back alone, trudging through the thorns by foot.

There is always a back stairs to magic, and it is just as well to keep it in mind, to know where it is and how to clamber down. The back stairs of aviation-magic is sometimes a parachute and sometimes a rubber life-boat. But it can also be a radio tube or a sextant or army rations or a life preserver or snake-bite serum or a bug-proof tent or a revolver or a compass—or even a pair of heavy boots. One must always be thinking, not only, "Thirteen hours of gasoline will take us to Aklavik," but also, "If we have an engine failure on the way, we have food enough for thirty days' walking to an outpost."

The back stairs are terribly important—almost more important than the front stairs—so much so that one is tempted to say, if it were not for them there could be no front stairs. For which reason I may be excused where I have emphasized the back stairs in my story.

For it is in an attempt to capture some of the magic that I have written this summer's experience—in an attempt to capture a phase in the history of travel that is perhaps unrepeatable and, as such, is worth being recorded.

For magic, unless it is written down, escapes one. Who would know, if it were not for Hans Andersen, that three enormous dogs, each bigger than the other, with eyes like saucepans, lay hidden in a tinder box; or that a pair of ordinary-looking galoshes could take one to the moon; or that if one sat on an old trunk and pressed the lock, one could hurtle across the skies anywhere?

"'Hurtle across the skies anywhere,'" someone repeats, smiling. "But that is no longer a fairy tale. That is almost everyday life!" Exactly, it is right on the line. Yesterday's fairy tale is today's fact. The magician is only one step ahead of his audience. I must write down my story before it is too late.

North to the Orient

ONE

North to the Orient

❊

To go north to the Orient is not a new venture. The idea must have originated soon after the discovery of America. That great "island" lying across the route foiled the schemes of early explorers who wanted to "saile by the West into the East." But there was still a chance of sailing by the *North* into the East. An attempt to find such a route may have been made as early as 1508 by Sebastian Cabot. And the Elizabethan explorers Frobisher and Davis, who followed him, started in earnest the long search for "a passage by the North-west to Cathaia."

In an age when continents were linked for the first time by boat, the trade lines to the East were the most important and eagerly sought. The Portuguese had already discovered and monopolized the route around Cape of Good Hope. Magellan had labored west across two oceans and through the straits to China. The Elizabethans, in Sir Hugh Willoughby's fatal expedition, had tried unsuccessfully to find a Northeast passage around Russia and Siberia, and were now turning in the other direction. They wanted a "new and nerer passage to Cataya," and their hope lay in the supposed straits on the north side of the recently discovered America.

Then, as now, the object of a new route was greater accessibility and speed. Cabot is quoted, in Hakluyt's *Voyages*, as saying, "If I should saile by way of the North-west, I should by a shorter tract come into India." Many explorers believed that if such a passage could be found "for the bringing of the Spiceries from

India into Europe," it would be the easiest and shortest of all routes.

There was, however, much doubt as to its existence. The problem attracted many minds to its study and drew earnest discussions from both sides. On the one hand, quotations from Greek philosophers, the legends of travelers, and the theories of cosmographers were all used to prove the existence of such a passage. On the other hand, learned men questioned the practicability of such a route. Expeditions had failed to find it. Cabot himself, according to the story, though he believed the passage to exist, was not successful in his search. Following the coast of America north, he became discouraged when it turned always to the east. Why should the Northwest not be as cold as the Northeast passage, the search for which had proved disastrous to Sir Hugh Willoughby? And even should they arrive at the "happy islands," after "so long, so painefull, so doubtfull a voyage by such a new found way," would the "Barbarians" trade with them? Would the winds and currents allow them to return?

The challenging spirit of the explorers rang in the answer:

"The rude Indian Canoa halleth those seas, the Portingals, the Saracenes, and Moores travaile continually up and downe that reach from Japan to China, from China to Malacca, from Malacca to the Moluccaes: and shall an Englishman, better appointed than any of them all feare to saile in that Ocean? What seas at all doe want piracie? what Navigation is there voyde of perill?"

But in spite of their courage they were not successful. No passage opened up before the eager boats of Martin Frobisher in 1576 or of John Davis who followed him. The hope of finding one continually increased. Frobisher's "Straight" was supposed to be the entrance. Each man felt that he came a little nearer to the goal. But there was always some unlooked-for accident or some distraction to turn him from his purpose: a mutiny, a storm, an attack from the savages, strong currents, islands of ice, exploration of the country itself or the search for gold. And the Northwest passage continued to be a golden myth, luring one expedition after another in its search, until in 1906 Amundsen's small sealing sloop finally reached Bering Strait and the Pacific Ocean, three years after it had left the Atlantic at Davis Strait. The myth had been proved a reality.

In the twentieth century we have turned to it again, not as a myth, a feat for explorers, or an undiscovered path toward an unknown end, but as a practical route to the Orient. For we are again approaching an age of new transoceanic routes, new ways to link countries and continents, this time by air. And the object is again greater accessibility and speed.

The great circle course ("the shortest surface distance between two points on a sphere") from New York to Tokyo points a straight line through Canada, and along the shores of the Arctic Sea, north to the Orient. This was the route we chose for our flight. The fact that it lay "in the edge of the frostie Zone" did not imply the hardship and danger for us that it had for the Elizabethans. Far from being a deterrent factor in our trip, it was rather a provocative one. For by crossing this zone we intended to save mileage and time. The Arctic, my husband remarked as we studied the globe, heretofore had been explored chiefly for its own interest. An Arctic air-route, although frequently discussed by explorers and aviators, had never been used primarily to shorten travel between the continents. It was Arctic air-routes, and the conditions to be encountered following them, which we hoped to study on our voyage to the Orient.

But why the Orient? one may ask. What led you to the Orient? Our immediate answer to such a question would be the indisputable importance of future airroutes between America and Japan, China and Siberia. And yet it is not quite a complete answer. For besides this main practical reason, there were others playing about it, under and over it, like a running accompaniment to the main theme in music—other small, personal, and trivial reasons, which, as they braided in and out of the main one ceaselessly, made of it a stronger bond, pulling us in one direction. These minor themes, these trivial reasons, capricious as swallows in their flight, are difficult to imprison with a name: and yet—if one tried to strke them down with words as missiles—they might be glanced at here and there by such terms as *color, glamour, curiosity, magic,* or *mystery.* For there is no other way of labeling the emotions which rise from scattered impressions throughout life: a Ming horse, the syllables *Marco Polo,* a silk kimono, the ragged head of a chrysanthemum, the color of a mandarin coat, and a petal-white bowl seen through the glass of a museum case. Irrelevant, slight impressions which, pieced together, make one's picture of the Orient alluring.

But not only our destination, our journey also was alluring. Aside from any practical aims and ends of the trip, and in spite of the inevitable difficulties, it was in itself fascinating. A fascination which has never been expressed better than by Master George Best in Hakluyt's *Voyages.* Writing an account of Frobisher's expeditions, he admits the difficulties of the life of the discoverer:

"How dangerous it is to attempt new Discoveries, either for the length of the voyage, or the ignorance of the language, the want of Interpretors, new and unaccustomed Elements and ayres, strange and unsavoury meates, danger of theeves and robbers, fiercenesse of wilde beastes and fishes, hugenesse of woods, dangerousnesse of Seas, dread of tempestes, feare of hidden rockes, steepnesse of mountaines, darkenesse of sudden falling fogges, continuall paines taking without any rest, and infinite others."

But in spite of these disadvantages, he goes on sanguinely to state the compensations:

"How pleasant and profitable it is to attempt new Discoveries, either for the sundry sights and shapes of strange beastes and fishes, the wonderfull workes of nature, the different maners and fashions of divers nations, the sundry sortes of government, the sight of strange trees, fruite, foules and beastes, the infinite treasure of Pearle, Golde, and Silver, the newes of newe found landes, the sundry positions of the Sphere, and many others."

And although we were not explorers in the Elizabethan sense, we can sympathize with their point of view. Travelers are always discoverers, especially those who travel by air. There are no signposts in the sky to show a man has passed that way before. There are no channels marked. The flier breaks each second into new uncharted seas.

And for us, setting out over unknown country, there would be those austere and breath-taking moments when, looking down on inaccessible territory, one realizes that no one has seen that spot before. It is as fresh, still, and untouched as the night's new-fallen snow. Unchanged from the day it was made. One looks terrified for a visible sign of piercing with the light of human eye the darkness of a hitherto unseen world. The intruding gaze, one feels, must make some mark or leave an impression, as a stone shatters the unbroken stillness of a pool.

Our route was new; the air untraveled; the conditions unknown; the stories mythical; the maps, pale, pink, and indefinite, except for a few names, far to the east of our course, to show that someone before us pointed his ship, also, "North to the Orient."

TWO

Preparation

❊

Flying implies freedom to most people. The average person who hears the drone of a motor and looks up from the walls of a city street to see an airplane boring its way through the clear trackless blue above—the average person, if he stops to use his imagination, may say to himself casually, "Free as a bird! What a way to travel! No roads—no traffic—no dust—no heat— just pick up and go!"

In that careless phrase he is apt to overlook what lies behind the word "free." He is apt to forget, or perhaps he never knew, the centuries of effort which have finally enabled man to be a bird, centuries of patient desiring, which reach back at least as far as the Greek world of Icarus. For Icarus, trying to scale the skies with his waxen wings, was merely an early *expression* of man's desire to fly. How long before him the unexpressed wish wrestled in the minds of men, no one can tell.

And since flight is not a natural function of man; since it has been won by centuries of effort; since it has been climbed to arduously, not simply stumbled upon; since it has been slowly built, not suddenly discovered, it cannot be suspended as the word "freedom" is suspended in the mind. It rests, firmly supported, on a structure of laws, rules, principles—laws to which plane and man alike must conform. Rules of construction, of performance, of equipment, for one; rules of training, health, experience, skill, and judgment, for the other.

Not only must a man know how his plane is made, what it will do, how it must be cared for; but also—to mention only a few of the rules that govern him—what the ceiling of his plane is, whether it will go high enough to clear any elevation on the route; what the

gas capacity is, how far it will carry him; what points
he can reach for refueling; how to navigate through a
signless sky; where he will land for the night; where
he can get emergency repairs; what weather conditions he may meet on his way; and, keeping in mind
the back stairs, what equipment he should carry in case
of a forced landing. All this he must know before he
can win that freedom of a bird, before he can follow
that straight line he has drawn on the map, directly,
without deviation, proverbially "as the crow flies."

The firm black lines which we ruled straight across
Canada and Alaska, preparatory to our flight, implied
a route which, in its directness of purpose and its
apparent obliviousness of outside forces, looked as
unerring and resistless as the path of a comet. Those
firm black lines implied freedom, actual enough, but
dearly won. Months, and indeed years, of preparation
made such freedom possible.

It is true that as air travelers we were free of many
of the difficulties that had beset the early surface travelers in search of a Northwest passage. Our fast mono-
plane could carry us far above most of the dangers
mentioned by Master George Best: "mountaines of
yce in the frozen Sea . . . fiercenesse of wilde beastes
and fishes, hugenesse of woods, dangerousnesse of
Seas, dread of tempestes, feare of hidden rockes."
But in any comparison between us and the early nav-
igators, there were disadvantages to offset advantages.

The early travelers, although confined to navigable
waters, and restricted by slow speed, nevertheless were
favored with a limitless fuel supply. Wherever they
went and no matter how long they were gone, they
could count on the wind for power. They might have
difficulties in using it, now coaxing it, now fighting it;
but they would never completely drain their supply.
It was inexhaustible. Whereas we must plan and
budget our fuel, arrange for its location along the route,
sometimes sending it ahead of us by boat or train, sometimes using fuel already cached through the North.

And although they had to be prepared for longer time, we must be prepared for greater space—north and south, sea and land—and therefore more varied conditions. Our equipment had to be as complete as theirs, and our carrying capacity was far more limited in weight as well as space.

Our craft, the *Sirius*, with its six-hundred-horse-power cyclone engine, was equipped with gasoline tanks which would carry us for two thousand miles, and with pontoons that would enable us to land in Hudson Bay, on the many inland lakes throughout Canada, along the coast of Alaska and Siberia, and among the Japanese islands. The general equipment had to include, among other things, instruments for blind flying and night flying; radio and direction-finding apparatus; facilities for fueling and for anchoring. (We had a twenty-five-pound anchor and rope tucked into a small compartment in the pontoons.) Aside from the general equipment indispensable for our everyday flying, we must carry a large amount of emergency supplies: an adequate repair kit and repair materials; a rubber boat, a sail and oars; an extra crash-proof, waterproof radio set; parachutes; general camping equipment and food supplies; firearms and ammunition; a full medicine kit; warm flying suits and boots; and many other articles.

The contingencies to be provided for were many and varied. We must consider the possibility of a parachute jump, and carry in our flying-suit pockets the most concentrated food and the most compact first-aid kit. We must be prepared for a forced landing in the North, where we would need warm bedding and clothes; and in the South, where we ought to have an insect-proof tent; and on the ocean, where we would need, in addition to food, plenty of fresh water.

And we must not exceed our limited weight budget. Every object to be taken had to be weighed, mentally as well as physically. The weight in pounds must balance the value in usefulness. The floor of our room for weeks before our departure was covered with large untidy piles of equipment. All day, while my husband was supervising the work on the plane, the piles had "Please do not disturb" signs on them. Each night they were rearranged. The things we had decided to take were heaped against one wall: rubber boat, flying suits, gloves, helmets, and stockings, pell-mell on top of each other. In the middle of the room were the baby's white scales and a large mountain of not-yet-decided-upon equipment. A third pile—by far the most untidy—of discarded things lay on the hearth.

I sat in the middle of the cans and read a book on calories, commenting from time to time, "Now, tomatoes haven't much food value, but they keep you from getting beri-beri. Magellan's men all got beri-beri, do you remember?" or, "Few calories in hardtack, but it will fill up the hole still left inside of you, after you've eaten your army rations for the day."

My husband added and subtracted endlessly from lists. "This shotgun would kill birds if we needed food; but each shell weighs nearly two ounces, and the gun itself weighs six pounds. Think what that would mean in food!"

"Or *shoes*," I said. Shoes are the most weight-expensive item in personal baggage. I tried to get along on two pairs. We allowed ourselves eighteen pounds each, including suitcase.

"I want a pair of shoes," I would say, entering a shop, "that I can wear at balls and dinners, and also at teas and receptions, and also for semi-sport dresses, and also for bedroom slippers."

"Anything else, Modom?" asked the bewildered clerk.

"Yes, I like low heels."

"Try our 'Growing-Girl' Department," he said, glad to get rid of me.

My preparation, however, did not consist alone in tracking down impossible shoes through "Growing-Girl" departments. The most important part of my work was learning to operate our radio. It started when my husband began explaining how safe the trip was going to be.

"Of course, we'll have to use pontoons instead of wheels up there," he remarked, studying the map of Canada, early in our preparations.

"Pontoons over all that dry land?" I queried.

"Yes, you can usually get down on a lake in northern Canada. The Canadian pilots always use seaplanes. And coming down the coast of Siberia, we could probably find sheltered water to land on—in an emergency we might even land in open ocean."

(Raised eyebrows, the only reply.)

"And if the ships got badly banged up," continued my husband, "we have the rubber boat."

"If we came down in the middle of the Bering Sea, Charles," I insisted, "it would be quite a long row to Kamchatka!"

"We might sail to shore, but otherwise we wouldn't have much chance of being found without radio," he agreed. And then firmly, "We'll have to carry radio."

"Can you operate radio?" (I can see it coming, I thought, I can just see what's going to happen.)

"A little—I learned at Brooks." (Then turning to me.) "But *you* will have to be radio operator."

"Oh!" (There it is! I thought.) "Well—I'll see."

The next day he came home with a small practice set of buzzers and keys, connected to two dry cells. When I pressed down the key, there was a little squeak which brought four dogs and the baby scrambling into my room. I went on boldly with the Morse code in front of me, and, like everyone with a new fountain-pen, spelling out my own name in dots and dashes: "Dit-darr, darr-dit, darr-dit, dit."

An experienced radio operator gave us practice in receiving in the evenings. It reminded me of French *dictées* in school, where, at first, I could copy all the words; then I stumbled over a hard one; finally, after struggling along, three or four words behind, I gave up in a panic, and let the dark torrent of language stream over me without trying to stem the tide.

In the meantime, my husband had been working with the experts of Pan American Airways over the installation of the radio equipment in the plane. We found that we would have to have a third-class license to operate other than emergency calls.

"Here it is," said my husband, reading out of a book of radio regulations, "'Applicants . . . must pass a code test in transmission and reception at a speed of fifteen words per minute in Continental Morse Code . . . and a practical and theoretical examination consisting of comprehensive questions on the care and operation of vacuum tube apparatus and radio communication laws and regulations.'"

"'Comprehensive questions on the care and operation of vacuum tube apparatus,'" I read over his shoulder.

"Now, Charles, you know perfectly well that I can't do that. I never passed an arithmetic examination in my life. I had to be tutored to get through elementary physics in college. I never understood a thing about electricity from the moment that man started rubbing sealing wax and fur!"

"It's too bad you didn't take more," he said heartlessly, "but it's not too late; we'll start tonight. I don't know much about radio; we'll work on it together."

We sat in front of clean pads and newly sharpened pencils that night.

"We might as well start with the vacuum tube," said our instructor.

"We might as well," I echoed, as one replies to the dentist's phrase, "We might as well start on that back wisdom tooth."

He began drawing hieroglyphic diagrams on the pad, and skipping through a rapid simple sketch of the theory. He was about to start on the second diagram.

"Just a moment," I said. "Before you leave that, *where* is the vacuum tube?"

The instructor's face wore an expression of incredulity, amazement, and then, simply, pity.

"Well, don't you see," he said very gently, as though talking to a child, "*This* is it," and then he started all over again.

"Oh, I see *now*," I said, elaborately emphatic, as though it were just a small detail he had cleared up. We went on to the next diagram. I knew my rôle now. It had a familiar swing, so often had I played it: to sit silent, confused, listening to long explanations which one pretended to understand because one could echo the last phrase said—"This in turn sets up a magnetic field in the tickler coil." The only beam of light in my dark mind was, as always, the thought—"I'll get it all explained to me after class."

This scheme worked very well. With the help of all of the diagrams, my college textbooks, and my husband's explanations, I managed to walk into the examination room one very hot day. I walked out before my husband; but I did not go as fully into the "Theory of regeneration in the vacuum tube." He passed with higher marks.

The practical end was on the whole easier. Long hours of work on the buzzer set in the silence of my bedroom gave me a kind of false confidence. The metallic *tick, tick, tick* of the key, against a background of chintz, rugs, and sofa pillows, seemed quite crisp and professional. This quality, however, quickly faded in the austere setting of a hangar. On the day of the radio test, the antenna was reeled out and hung on a rafter. An unknown radio operator somewhere on Long Island had agreed to listen for us. I called him shakily, three times. My own sending hissed in the ear-phones. Would I forget the letters? No, they sprang instinctively from my fingers as I read them from the notebook. "Who - - - is - - - at - - - the - - - key?" came back the answer. I had to write down the letters as fast as they came. Still a beginner, my mind heard only single letters, and could not retain whole words.

"Anne - - - Lindbergh - - - how - - - is - - - this - - - sending?" I scribbled on my pad and then tapped out. My fingers could not yet read directly from my mind, but only from the written word on the paper.

"Pretty - - - good - - -" the letters ran slowly into words as I copied, "but - - - a - - - little - - - heavy - - - on - - - the - - - dashes—" (It seemed intensely funny to me, this slow deliberate conversation with a strange person somewhere on Long Island.) "—just - - - like - - - my - - - wife's - - - sending."

I smiled in the cockpit. How strange to feel you knew an unknown man from a single phrase over the radio—"just like my wife's sending!" I could hear the tone of his voice, the inflection, the accent on the *my,* the somewhat querulous, somewhat weary, somewhat kindly and amused, somewhat supercilious, husbandly tone—"just like *my* wife's sending." Yes, decidedly, there was still a good deal for me to learn.

We thought we were rather well along in our preparations. My husband had been in contact with the State Department in Washington. Gasoline was located along the routes; the pontoons were completed; we had installed a radio of the type used on the South American routes of Pan American Airways; and we were third-class radio operators. But we realized how little we had done when, the morning after the announcement was made of our trip, the newspapers voluntarily flooded us with information. Our routes, stops, distances, and fuel consumption were all accurately planned out for us. (Who, I thought sympathetically, did all that arithmetic in such a short time? I detest turning gas into RPM—revolutions per minute—and RPM into miles.) Someone had gleaned all the statistics for years about weather, winds, and flying conditions across the Arctic. Someone else had ferreted out all known travelers, by foot, ship, train, or plane to Canada, Alaska, Siberia, Japan, and China, and gathered together all the information they had to give. Guidebooks, travelers' diaries, and encyclopedias must have been open long past midnight for that great body of tourist information. "What the Lindberghs will see." "What the Lindberghs should see." "What might interest them." Somebody must have spent sleepless nights for all this. I felt quite guilty as I sat down in a comfortable chair and read about "the hairy Ainus, wild inhabitants of the Chishima Islands" and "primitive Eskimos who suck the eyes out of raw fish."

It was just as well that I read about them—I never saw any.

THREE
Take-Off

❁

The twenty-seventh of July, 1931, was clear and hot. The heat of a whole summer was condensed dripping into that afternoon. A small crowd of people pressed tightly against the gates to the long ramp at College Point, Long Island. As we drove in I saw many familiar faces between movie-tone trucks and cameras. We had all spent sweltering days together on that wooden ramp, watching trial flights and the installation of equipment. Now the preparation was over, we were ready to go. I suppose they were as relieved as we. Friends came up to say good-by. "We all hope you are going to get through it all right," with voices and expressions that said, "But we don't think you've got much chance."

Picking up our baggage, we hurried into the shade of the factory office. A dark heavy heat hung over everything. Men in shirt sleeves ran in and out. We could hear reporters telephoning, "Just arrived in brown auto—now packing up the plane." I turned around; little boys were looking in the window at me and giggling. I mopped my face and counted my radio pads and pencils. A reporter poked his head in the door. "Can't you even say you think it is an especially dangerous trip, Mrs. Lindbergh?" he asked.

I laughed, "I'm sorry, I really haven't anything to say." (After all we want to go. What good does it do to talk about the danger? "What navigation is there voyde of perill?" . . . "What navigation—")

"But, Mrs. Lindbergh, we would like to get some impressions from you. What is it you dread most? What—" A kind friend repeated that I did not want to talk. It was too hot to talk, anyway. It was too hot to sit down. I leaned against the shiny cool-looking surface of a desk.

As I walked out of the building two women ran up to me.

"Oh, Mrs. Lindbergh," said one, "the women of America are so anxious to know about your clothes."

"And I," said the other, "want to write a little article about your housekeeping in the ship. Where do you put the lunch boxes?"

I felt depressed, as I generally do when women reporters ask me conventionally feminine questions. I feel as they must feel when they are given those questions to ask. I feel slightly insulted. Over in the corner my husband is being asked vital masculine questions, clean-cut steely technicalities or broad abstractions. But I am asked about clothes and lunch boxes. Still, if I were asked about steely technicalities or broad abstractions, I would not be able to answer, so perhaps I do not deserve anything better.

"No," I said. "I'm sorry, but I really haven't anything to say." (What could I say that would have any significance? All the important questions about the trip will be answered by my husband.)

"But you must not disappoint all the people who are so anxious to hear about you. You know, the American Public—"

(—will be disappointed if they don't know where I put the lunch boxes! You aren't going to ask me to believe that, I thought.)

"I'm sorry, I'm very sorry."

I turned to look at the plane. Perched on top of the big pontoons, it seemed small and dainty. They were rolling it down the pier. I thought of all the emergency equipment for North and South, land and water, all parts of the world, packed into that little space. I thought of the two of us, ready to go in it anywhere, and I had a sense of our self-contained insularity. Islands feel like this, I am sure, and walled cities, and sometimes men.

It was ready now; we could get in. "No, thank you, I don't need a ladder to climb up." A mechanic was just clambering out of my cockpit. I had a moment to wait and watch the crowd. A radio announcer was speaking into his microphone. "Mrs. Lindbergh," he started smoothly, with a glance at me, "is wearing a leather flying helmet and leather coat, and high leather flying boots."

"Why!" I thought blankly, looking down at a costume which did not correspond at all to his description. What nonsense! It was much too hot to wear leather. The sun beat down on my bare head and sticky cotton blouse; the hot planks of the pier burned through my thin rubber sneakers. What made him say that, I wondered. Oh, of course, it isn't the conventional flying costume. They have to say that I am dressed in leather. I see, you needn't bother to tell me again, I thought, looking at the announcer. I know, "The Great Radio Public must not be disappointed!"

The spray sluiced over the windshield as we started to take off—faster now—we were up on the step— we were trying to get off the water. I held my breath after each pounding spank as the pontoons skipped along from wave to wave. Weighed down with its heavy test load of fuel, the plane felt clumsy, like a duck with clipped wings. It met the coming wave quivering after each effort to rise. Now the spanks were closer together—quick, sharp jolts. I put my hand on the receiving set. It was shaking violently. Suddenly all vibration smoothed out. Effortlessly we rose; we were off; a long curve upward. The squat ferryboats below plowed across our wake, and great flat barges carrying rectangular mounds of different colored earth like spools of gold and tawny silk. I found the little black mass of people on the pier where we had been. Small and insignificant it looked, now I could see the whole life of the river: many piers and crowded ferryboats, ships and roofs and fields and barges, dredges and smokestacks and the towers of New York. We looked insignificant, also, and small to them, I knew, now that our bulk on the end of the pier no longer blocked the horizon. It had become simply a boat in the river of many boats; then a plane in the sky with other planes; now, only a speck against the blue, mistaken easily for a gull.

The photographer's ship banked under us and vanished. Our flight had begun. We were on our way to Washington for our final clearances and passports. I must start working on the radio. WOA at North Beach was waiting for my first message. "First see that the correct coils are in place." I knew the directions by heart. Slowly I let down the door which opened the transmitting set, and took out the two coils which were there. MO was printed on the back of one; PA, on the other. *Master Oscillator* and *Power Amplifier*—I knew those names anyway. They were such nice satisfactory names, one always jingling along rhythmically after the other—*Master Oscillator* (pause) *Power Amplifier*. They seem to belong inevitably together like Tweedledum and Tweedledee or Arabella and Araminta, and to complement each other like question and answer. Master Oscillator? Power Amplifier. I held them in my lap, as there was no other place to put them. They were both marked 5615 KC. That was not the right frequency. I was planning to send on 3130 kilocycles, therefore I must find the 3130 coils in the coil box at my feet. Feeling blindly, I took out two at random. (Later I could pick the correct coils by feeling them, as, for example, 500 had the most turns of fine wire.) They turned out to be 500 KC. These also went on my lap. Four more came out. One of the coils fell down and started rolling back into the dark unknowns of the fuselage. I stretched after it and picked up 3130. When I finally had the 3130's plugged in, I started to put the other coils back in the box. It was like trying to fit a lamp's plug into a socket in the dark. First I pushed them down with calm assurance. They would not slip in. Then I carelessly tried to jiggle them in, then scraped them along the whole box, trying to find the holes. I became very hot. Suppose I could not get them in? Would I have to hold them all the way to Washington? What would my instructor say—and all the newspapers! "Mrs. Lindbergh did not do any radio sending because she could not fit the coils into their places."

Power Amplifier—Master Oscillator—I looked at them side by side and suddenly noticed the plugs were placed differently. Power Amplifiers fitted into one side of the box; Master Oscillators, into the other side. (Arabella had a blue hair ribbon, Araminta had a pink hair ribbon, in the nursery tale. I remembered now.) How simple.

"Next unwind the antenna to the proper resonance point." (Approximately forty-eight reel turns for 3130 KC, my direction book read.) I counted forty-eight very carefully. I didn't trust myself to find the correct resonance point by experimentation. Then I practiced my message without turning the switch on the keyboard. The message had been written half an hour earlier, before my adventures with the coils. It

read, "Now passing Newark Airport." I would have to
change that to, "Nearing Philadelphia." I turned on
the switch and called three times to WOA. A buzzing
silence followed. Again. No results. I repeated frequently. Something must be wrong. Something quite
simple; probably there was a main switch off. I hunted
around and found another switch on the dynamotor,
and turned it on. I tried to call again. Same result. I
reeled the antenna in and out to be sure I had counted
the turns correctly. The bulbs were burning in both
sets. I remembered something about a knife-switch
in the transmitter. "Should be closed when in the air
to shunt out a resistance"—whatever that meant. I
opened the transmitter and reached for the knife switch
—something hit me in the chest! A shock. I remembered now—400 volts. My husband handed back a
canteen of water and a note saying that there must be
a "short" somewhere, and telling me to take out the
fuses.

"I would if I knew what a fuse looked like."

He showed me a spare one. I took out the fuses and
sat subdued for the rest of the flight. Someone had
once told me that I was incredibly stupid in mechanical
things. Everyone would say it was because I was a
woman. Perhaps it was. If I were a failure at radio
there would be plenty of time to think about lunch
boxes and clothes.

"Don't look so gloomy," read the next note. "Probably due to a short circuit when they installed the compass light—get it fixed at North Beach on our way to
Maine. Anyway, the radio isn't important from New
York to Washington. Very good weather, too."

I looked out. We were circling over the Potomac
River and our anchorage, the little inlet behind Bolling
Field. Calm waters mirrored the breathless willows.
Our first day's flying was over.

North Haven

❋

The flight from New York to Washington marked the beginning of our journey. For me, however, the trip did not really begin until we said good-by to my home in Maine. Landing in North Haven satisfied that inner necessity, inherited from childhood games, of touching "home base" before starting out on a new race. The visit was an emotional springboard, and, as such, was marked with an importance far greater than its brief hours might warrant. The journey from New York to Maine, the few hours on the island, the good-bys, were all weighed down with a coating of many summers' impressions and emotions, besides those of the moment. It was one of those strange flashing seconds in life when you can draw the strands of the past and the future together in your hand and tie them firmly in a knot. For, as I visualize that summer's flight, stretching like a taut string over the top of the globe, the knotted end is held fast in North Haven.

The trip to Maine used to be a long and slow one. There was plenty of time in the night, spattered away in the sleeper, in the morning spent ferrying across the river at Bath, in the afternoon syncopated into a series of calls on one coast town after another—there was plenty of time to make the mental change coinciding with our physical change. Our minds could quietly step across the connecting passage from city to country, from school to vacation, from winter to summer. In the afternoon, when the train, like a busy housewife, did not have time to stop and chatter long to each station, but could not pass one by without a friendly puff and a nod, as each town showed us a typically Maine land-mark—a harbor full of little boats all pulling at their buoys, a white steeple, or a field of daisies—we were reminded of and prepared for our own harbor and field and steeple. As we neared our geographical destination we were also nearing our emotional one. The last lap of the journey across to the island by small boat completed both of these ends and each familiar personal landmark, drawing from us always the same exclamations—"The four-masted schooner is still there!" "Isn't that the five-mile buoy?" "There's our big spruce tree!"—linked us at last completely and satisfactorily to all past summers—to all vacations and to Maine.

But on this swift flight to North Haven in the *Sirius* my mind was so far behind my body that when we flew over Rockland Harbor the familiar landmarks below me had no reality. It took my mind overnight to catch up again and I lost much of the usual joy of arrival. I have had this sensation in flying many times before—this lack of synchronization of the speeds of mind and body. Pessimistically I have wondered if rapid transportation is not robbing us of the realization of life and therefore much of its joy. But I have decided that we are like the nearsighted man who is not yet used to his new spectacles. We are still trying to look at the stamen of a flower with spectacles made to look at horizons. Our children will measure their distances not by steeples and pine trees but by mountains and rivers. And these landmarks will mean as much emotionally to them as the four-masted schooner in Rockland Harbor did to me.

The impression of unreality was increased for me on this trip because I had worked hard on the radio, my head bent down in the cockpit all the way. It could not be called a successful afternoon, because of my inexperience in dealing with static and a kind of stage fright which froze my mind and ears whenever I heard a message dancing toward me. However, I was encouraged because I took down several garbled lines from both New York and Bangor, Maine, and kept sending out our position reports with regularity and optimism.

Even when we had actually landed and were anchored in the thoroughfare at North Haven I was still intent on getting a last message through to North Beach. And when, in the middle of this work, my husband said, "Your father and mother are over there in the next boat," I did not even look up. "Yes—yes, I know," I said impatiently, and pocketed my joy as one pockets a long-awaited letter brought in public—a letter whose very handwriting jumps from the page though one only says, paradoxically, "It's nothing, it can wait."

It seemed to me when we finally started toward the dock that all of North Haven was either rowing around in the thoroughfare or jammed on to the landing. But the crowd did not affect me as other crowds. All the faces seemed familiar, North Haven citizens and summer vacationists. Even the ones I did not know bore family resemblances to the others—perhaps just the resemblance that the same occupations give to people, or the same physical bloom from salt and sun. I felt my usual costume of restraint fall off me as though stepping into my own family. These friends had known me so long; they had seen me come in from a cold sail a hundred times with a red nose and blowy hair. They had watched my confusion and misery when I backed the old Buick into the ditch and somebody's fence. They had pulled me out too. There was no mystery about me for them to peer curiously for. I would not disappoint or thrill them. Even for my husband there was a different kind of curiosity. Of course they all wanted to see him, and they would not have missed it for anything. But, after all, he could not really be such a mysterious person. Hadn't he married Anne? I felt intensely relieved and happy. How delicious to step into one's old wrapper and bedroom slippers. I was at home.

I was not really at home, though, until I had gone over every room in that white-clapboard house and placed again in my memory every picture on the wall and every object on the mantel until the Audubon prints stopped jumping out to meet me every time I entered the living room, and the Toby on the dining-room mantel did not nod at me when I sat down to a meal. After all the inanimate things that make up a room had given me their preliminary welcome and had settled back into their familiar and inconspicuous niches —then I was fully at home.

We sat that night in the warm glow of a fire of ques-tions and exclamations: "How is the radio going?" "Static? That's what we said this afternoon." "How long will it take to Ottawa?" "Those maps you gave us are grand, Charles." My husband never answered any questions about radio, even when he knew the answer far better than I did. He would just turn to me with the expression half proud and half anxious that a mother wears talking to her performing child, "Speak up now, Anne, say your piece for the gentlemen." But I had the satisfaction of realizing that, if I knew far less than my husband, my family, impossible as it might seem, knew even less than I. They looked really im-pressed when I said that I had mixed up the Power Amplifier with the Master Oscillator coils.

The next morning we were off again, I with an extra handkerchief tucked into my pocket. "You will prob-ably need an extra one, you know." That extra hand-kerchief seemed to set a seal of success on the trip. It made it at once intimate and possible. Hadn't an extra handkerchief taken me to school and back, and put me on the train for college, and sent me out the day I was married? One could go anywhere with an extra handkerchief—especially if it had a blue border.

The day was hard and clear and bright, like the light slanting off a white farmhouse. The island falling away under us as we rose in the air lay still and perfect, cut out in starched clarity against a dark sea. I had the keenest satisfaction in embracing it all with my eye. It was mine as though I held it, an apple in my hand. All the various parts of it were mine at the same moment; the crowd on the pier, the little rocking boat in the harbor where my family waved, the white farmhouse on the point where my baby was. What a joy to hold them all in my eyes at once, as one tries, saying good-by to a person, to possess all of them in one look. The different parts of the island, also, which had once been many complicated worlds, were joined together and simplified by this enveloping glance from the air. "So the 'Cat-Farm-Road' really is a continuation of 'Round-the-Point Road'!" I found myself saying. "And the lily pond is just on the other side of the golf course. How strange! And it seemed such a long walk that day."

I had great pleasure in straightening these confusions in my mind, in clarifying the complexities of my childhood world. And this sense of detachment in space gave me also a sense of detachment in time, as though I were looking back at my own life from some high point in the future—as though I could even look back on the trip we had not yet made, and from my vantage point say calmly, "How strange, I thought it would be so long—so difficult, that summer—and really—"

FIVE

Radio and Routes

❀

To add to my happiness, on the trip from North Haven to Ottawa I had my first successful day at the radio. I was in contact with one or the other of two stations every fifteen minutes of the trip. I was able to send out our "Posn" (position) and "Wea" (weather) regularly, and to hear in return the comforting "dit-darr-dit" (r) which means "received ok." On the other hand, when I look over the notes now, I am surprised at the number of times I had to send "Sorry pse rpt" (Sorry please repeat) or "Sorry agn pse" (Sorry again please).

I discovered on this trip, to my great disappointment, that receiving was not so simple as my experience with our parlor radio had led me to believe. It had always before merely been a matter of pressing a switch, turning a knob to a well-smudged pencil mark, where there was a blast of music, made softer by turning another knob. That was all there was to it. I sat back lazily while the music, or something else, stayed there obediently as long as I wished. On this airplane receiver I had also marked the dial for the different stations on their various frequencies, and I imagined that all I had to do was to press the switch, find my station, and, after a little adjusting, simply sit back and listen. But the dots and dashes refused to stay on my pencil mark. I found I needed one hand constantly on the main dial, another on the vernier, trying to pin down my station like an elusive butterfly. I wanted a third to write the message, and still another to hold the pad—the work of four hands to be done by two incompetent ones. That meant acrobatics.

The chief trouble was that I was still at a painfully slow stage of radio operating. When I was first learning to take down messages, my mind seized on the sound of a single set of dots and dashes, translated it hesitatingly into a letter, and immediately ejected it to make room for the next. It was not possible to hold more than one set in my mind at once. In order not to forget them I had to write down the letters one by one as they were translated, and to piece out the words and meaning afterward. Gradually I seemed to eliminate the middle step, and the sound of a letter dictated directly to my fingers without, apparently, passing through my mind at all. Letters flowed from the pencil to the tune of dots and dashes, like spirit writing. But even then, I did not know what the message was until it was over and I could read it on my scratch pad.

simile

While this method was an improvement on the earlier one, it still had many drawbacks. Like the magician who was powerless without his wand, I was completely at the mercy of my pencil and really could not hear without one in my hand. Later I found my mind stepped back into the process. It began first to retain letters; next to anticipate words; and then with certain words not to be conscious at all of the letters, but to hear only words as the signals came in, as though I were listening to a conversation. Taking the message thus, by ear alone, would leave my right hand momentarily free to adjust the reception controls, which were on the right side of the cockpit. But on the trip to Ottawa, and for a long time afterward, I had no free right hand. It had to hold the magic pencil, which, unfortunately, lost its magic when held in the left.

I managed, however, to do fairly well in an awkward-appearing position. My right hand took messages on a pad balanced on my left knee, while my left hand crossed over and controlled the dials at my right. An expert pianist sometimes looks like this, playing bass with his right hand and treble with his left, but an expert radio operator never should. Sometimes, tiring of this cross-armed position, I sat on the floor, facing my receiving set. This position was satisfactory as long as I was receiving, but if I wanted to send, the transmitting key was perfectly placed only for the occupant of the seat. I could not reach it from the floor. There was no use trying to get around the fact that the radio equipment was installed for a radio operator. I would simply have to learn to be a radio operator. I felt more like one, even though I looked like a pianist, by the time I reached Ottawa, and proudly sent out, as my last message, our position over the city. The answer came back slowly and gently, "OK - - - better - - - reel in - - - antenna." My patient instructor at the other end was sending a last thoughtful reminder. Yes, I thought, as we skimmed swiftly down over the broad satin of the Ottawa River, perhaps he was right.

Still fresh from my first practical experience as an operator, I was slightly ruffled when told, on our arrival at Ottawa, that I was to sit at dinner next to one of the foremost experts on radio in the country. "He is a man," it was explained to me with cordial enthusiasm, "who knows all there is to know in this field. You can just have a splendid talk about everything." All thoughts left my mind at that moment, as when some member of your family shouts into the long-distance telephone the chilling words, "Anne is right here and wants to speak to you." And the mouthpiece, like a hot plate, is dropped into your lap. What would I say to a radio expert? "My husband——" I started lamely. But this would not do. "Your husband says you have entire charge of the radio." ("Speak up now, Anne.") I went in to dinner, coaching myself sternly, "Don't say *coil* when you mean *tube*, and try not to speak at all."

In the meantime my husband was having his own discussion with experts. An absorbed group of aviators, travelers, explorers, meteorologists, surveyors, and scientists—men who knew Northern Canada as no other group in the world—stood around him arguing. In front of them were spread the charts on which our marked routes cut heavy black lines, definite and simple as the meridians, straight across "the wilds of Canada." The floor was strewn with different colored maps, photographs, and lists of statistics. But the experts were looking at the heavy black lines on our charts when I slipped into the back of the room. They looked troubled. It was a look of wisdom and kindness covered with restraint—the look your mother wore when you came in to say good-by to her before one of your first parties. You remember, although she said loyally, "You look lovely, dear," you knew she was thinking, "But *why* did you wear *that* dress?"

"*Why* (very gently and politely)—why did you choose *that* route, sir?"

"Well—it's the shortest."

Yes, it was the shortest. There was nothing to say to that argument. It was going to be hard to talk reasonably to this man.

"But not very much shorter, sir, than this route up the Mackenzie River—and—there's nothing to see up in that Hudson Bay country."

"I wouldn't give two cents for that country," chimed in another Canadian. "I've been all over it—nothing but swamps—not a camp or a hut for hundreds of miles."

"And these places you've marked for stops—there's no one there—no place to stay—only a Hudson's Bay post or a Mounted Police station—"

There was a gleam in my husband's eye. That was not the way to discourage him. "Well?" he said, smiling provocatively.

"Well, sir (Really, this man was making it difficult!), these river mouths aren't safe at all to anchor in. There is a tremendous tide up in Hudson Bay. You think your ship is holding nicely in the harbor, and you find the next morning it's dragged anchor and gone out to sea."

"Or else you're anchored in an inlet and the tide goes out, leaving you high and dry."

"And the pontoons are apt to sink down and stick in the quicksand, so that when the tide comes back you're submerged."

"And then, sir, there are bad fog conditions up there. Fog—and glass water—so that a pilot can't see where the water is at all. He runs right into it—very dangerous!"

"The magnetic pole will throw your compass out, you know?"

"And the mosquitoes—my word—you can't get your shoes on for bites."

To this avalanche of objections, some outsider could not resist saying, "Well, *you* all got back alive, didn't you?"

There was no answer to that argument either, except laughter. But the experts had a heavy responsibility. They were not going to give up without a little more effort.

"Now this jump here, sir—I wouldn't take *my* wife over that. Mrs. Lindbergh—"

I felt strangely flattered as I did the first time I walked into an elevator and a man took off his hat for me. (Have I then, I thought, incredulous at fifteen, reached that important age when men take off their hats for me!)

"You must remember," my husband parried, with a smile at me, "that *she* is *crew*."

And I felt even more flattered. (Have I then reached a stage where I am considered on equal footing with men!)

"But with this wonderful route right alongside here, *why* should you choose to go up over that terrible country?"

I watched with amusement. They talked to my husband as older people to a little boy who wants to play with firecrackers, "Now these sparklers are just as exciting and much prettier."

"Such a beautiful route, sir, you'd enjoy it much more."

"But we don't want to go along organized air-routes."

"Oh, it's no organized air-route. It will be plenty wild enough for you, and just a few miles longer."

"I like to feel that in flying"—my husband faced them—"I can mark one point on the map for my position and another point for my destination, and that I can draw a straight line between the two, and follow it. I don't like to deviate for possible difficulties en route. I'd rather prepare for the difficulties."

The situation was becoming a little tense. The "small boy" was evidently serious. The experienced older pilots looked at him with some doubt and much embarrassment. How could they explain to him the difficulties? They began to skate dangerously near certain holes in the ice: "We can't take the responsibility—if something happens to you—international complications—"

"All right," snapped back the answer. "If we can't take that route (Careful, careful, Charles!), we'll go back and go over Greenland!"

Many long faces. "Well, that's worse!" Everyone laughed. The general attitude was: if he *has* to play with firecrackers—we've done our best to dissuade him—he might as well be shown how. And that they proceeded to do with a generosity we did not deserve after all the trouble we had given them.

"If you *do* go, sir, you don't have to land always in inlets. There are lots of little inland lakes, a mile or so from the port, where you will be quite safe from tide and current."

"And you may find these photographic maps useful. They show the anchorage."

"We'll get you some wing-ropes—no, no bother, and you'll have to take two of our life preservers. You can't get them anywhere else."

"And there's just one thing, sir, we know you'll get through all right!"

SIX

Baker Lake

❀

All afternoon we had flown over miles and miles of perfectly flat treeless land, mottled with lakes and marshes. Toward evening we came upon a gray glassy lake, bounded by gray bleak shores a little higher than the marshes. And on shore, the only points of accent in that monotonous landscape, stood three or four white houses. This was Baker Lake. We circled over the flagpole, the British flag, the church steeple, and cut across the dull satin water of the lake to the little group of people on shore. As we pushed near the sandy bank I had a closer view of the land, gray again—no trees, no hills, nothing but gray moss, gray water, and a gray sky. How could anything live there, even animals? For this was the trading post. There, on the shore ahead of us, was a small white shack with the sign "Revillon Frères Ltd. Furs." The same fine flowing script, the same curves and flourishes, the same style that marks the big store in New York. Rumbling busses, barking taxis, the wheeze of brakes as the animals halt, checked by the red lights, the growls as they spring forward again—all roaring Fifth Avenue lay in that sign, "Revillon Frères."

animal imagery

My husband switched off the motor. The propeller clicked around idly and stopped. There was no noise except the lapping of our wash against the sand. The group of men on shore, a few white men, and Eskimos in pointed Santa Claus hoods, came forward. The Canadian Mounted officer, tall and handsome in his red coat, put out a hand to us. "We've reserved tickets for the show tonight. I hope you'll come!"

"What's that?" said my husband, not knowing whether to laugh or not, as he looked at the four lone houses. Great guffaws from the group.

When I jumped out, the three or four Eskimos drew back. Then two little Eskimo boys came up shyly and followed me about. Their bright eyes shone under their caps as they searched my face and costume curiously.

"You see," explained one of the traders, "you're the first white woman they've ever seen. There's never been one here before."

"And what a disappointment I must be," I said, looking down at my clothes. "I've got trousers on just like the rest of you!"

It was damp and muggy. The mosquitoes buzzed

in a cloud around our heads and I envied the Eskimos their cloth hoods. We ran heavily through the sand into the small square house. The sitting room with bright curtains, a couch, a big table, and chairs; a small bedroom, with clothes curtained off at one end; a little closet room for the radio; and an outside porch, where two Eskimos helped with the work: this made up the house. We sat around the big table for supper with the two traders as our hosts.

"Sorry we can't give you anything better," they said, "but our boat is due about now and we're pretty short."

"Your boat?"

"Our boat from home—comes in once a year, you know—all our supplies."

We looked rather shocked. "I thought planes dropped in here once in a while. At Ottawa they said—"

"Oh, that was a long time ago. Haven't had supplies in here since our boat left last year. Well—we have enough, you know." They set down some fresh salmon trout in front of us. "This comes out of the lake—lots of fish—but you get awfully tired of it. No fresh vegetables or fruit."

How deprived I always felt without fruit or a green vegetable at every meal! Even on flying trips I tried to take fruit instead of sandwiches. Why, at Ottawa, there was some tucked in my radio bag. Reaching into it, I pulled out three plums, a pear, and four meat sandwiches.

"These aren't very good but if you'd like them?"

The two men smiled and thanked us. "I guess this is the first fresh beef that's ever been up here." Very seriously they sat down and cut up the food into equal parts. When it was divided each had his share of our three-day-old sandwiches and fruit while we feasted on fresh salmon.

Before supper was finished the others stamped in—

two Hudson's Bay men from across the lake, the red-coated "Mounted," a Canadian game warden, and an Anglican parson. They nodded taciturnly, sat down around the edge of the room, and stared at us.

"What's it like *outside?*"

We hesitated a moment before answering. The peculiar emphasis on that word "*outside*." They could not mean the weather.

"Our newspapers are a year old," explained one of them. "We get three hundred and sixty-five at a time, and read one every day—just as you do at home—only, of course, the news is a year late."

Like the mythical man on the star, I thought, with a mythical telescope, who, because light takes one hundred years to travel there from the earth, sees the Civil War a century after it happened.

"We get news over the radio," went on another, "but nobody here's been *outside* for a year. I've been in six."

"I'm the latest arrival," said the parson. His scrubbed face shone over a stiff collar. "I came in a year ago, and I'm up for seven," he laughed jovially.

So the rest of the world was *outside* and Baker Lake was *inside*. They talked about it as a prison.

"He's up for five," another remarked, "and that man there—he's 'bushed.'" They all laughed. "Came in nine years ago—signed up for five—couldn't stand it when he got outside again—now he's signed up for five more."

"The Padre's in for life." The Padre was a Roman Catholic priest we had met on the beach as we landed. A red prophet's beard fell over his long black gown. He was not there that evening because he and the parson were not on speaking terms. They seldom met, even on those timeless winter evenings when the little colony gathered around the big table to play "rummy" or bridge. There were only eight of them, but as the parson did not believe in playing cards he broke up the second table. The Padre played, however. He knew what existence was like in the North. He was there for life.

How difficult it must be, I thought, avoiding someone in that small community, especially for two engaged in the same work. It seemed to me there were only about two tentfuls of Eskimos. I wondered how they divided up the converts. The former Anglican missionary, we learned, had been very popular with the Eskimos and had won all of them to his side. The Catholic priest had only one follower (and he had once been an Anglican), the man whom he hired to work for him. "And what else could the poor chap do?" was the comment. The parson had a good head start in the new struggle and six years ahead of him. Still, the Padre would probably win out in the end. He was there for life.

I looked around at the group. The Factor was nudging the man next to him and laughing. The parson's face shone like an apple. The "Mounted" was turning a handmade cigarette of pipe tobacco in his fingers, sticking the paper together with his tongue (all last year's cigarettes were used up). They did not look like exiles.

"You must get a lot of news from the radio?" we asked.

"Yes—it's good in the winter"—he stopped turning his cigarette—"but it's rather a shame; in the old days after you were once here you couldn't get any more orders from headquarters! Now they can get you any Saturday night."

They all laughed at this. So they wanted to be exiles—"bushed," they called it, unable to leave the country they once thought they couldn't live in. And yet they wanted "news from home." "Home"—I realized we did not come from "home." Home meant different parts of Canada to some of them, Scotland and England to others; and we had no news. I dragged my memory for some thread of association we could follow together. I had lived in Scotland one summer, at North Berwick, near Edinburgh. A rosy-faced man beamed at me. "That would be next to the big golf course, wouldn't it?"

"Yes—we were right on the golf course. Do you remember the Law?" (The "Law" was a mountain.)

The others looked at us with surprised envy and we felt warm pride to find this island to meet on, in a sea of unsimilarity.

"You've never been to England, Mrs. Lindbergh?" interrupted another of the group.

"Why, yes, I have, but I've never lived there." He looked disappointed. "But my sister is there now," I went on, as though by that tenuous link to draw him nearer England. "She is in Somerset."

"Somerset," he repeated. And then quite wistfully, "Has she ever been to Devon?" What difference did it make to him whether my sister had ever been to Devon? None, I suppose. But to mention a loved object, a person, or a place to someone else is to invest that object with reality. You say the magic word: the listener smiles, an image forming in his thoughts, and then, as though his image were superimposed upon yours, a picture rises out of the dark sea of memory— not the flat photograph which has hung so long on the walls of his mind that it has lost meaning, but a new picture with depth and life and solidity, as though seen through a stereoscope. Perhaps it is a mental stereo-scope, made with the combination of his vision and yours.

So I answered him and said she had once sent me a postcard from Clovelly. And he was pleased.

Just then there was a shuffle of feet in the hall out-side. Lynn, the trapper, stood in the door. "Hello there!" They all greeted him jovially. He himself said nothing, nodded good-naturedly, pulled off a mackinaw and sat down. His blue eyes squinted at us as though still staring at the snow, in which he lived so much of the year. For Lynn was a veteran trapper, a great burly

Swede, who had spent his life in the North. For years he had set his traps in the timber lands of Canada. But it was getting too crowded now, he said, so he moved north. Too crowded! I thought of our flight from Ottawa to Moose Factory: battalions of pine trees marching north in straight lines, steadily advancing as far as one could see, and not a town or a house or a puff of smoke to stop their even pace. Was all that land staked out, covered by trappers in the winter? Perhaps. Anyway, it was too crowded for Lynn.

Here, at least, he had no interference. He lived eighteen miles out of the Baker Lake camp, they told us, in a hut he himself had built out of mud and a few boards dragged from the camp. It was just long enough to lie down in. All winter long, trapping and hunting with his dog, with an occasional hike on snowshoes into camp for supplies: this was Lynn's life as they described it to us. I do not remember his saying anything. He sat in the corner, a cap drawn over his face, a creased, weather-beaten face, but warm and familiar as an old leather glove—his blue eyes squinting at us as though still staring at the snow.

It was the *winter* they were all waiting for, and winter work. It is work just to live out of doors then, with traffic by snowshoe and dog sled, when even for the hardest exercise—running by the side of the dogs —one must be wrapped in deerskin. It was in the winter that all the work of trapping fell, for the fox coats were heavier and more beautiful. Some of the men went out over the snow on their own trap lines, others waited for the Eskimos to come back with skins which were traded in at the "store."

The "store" was the shack on the beach we had seen on landing. It was the most important building there and we were taken through it the next morning. Here, on shelves lining the walls of the small front room, were stacked all kinds of supplies: cans of meat, vegetables, and soup; sweaters, caps, and underwear; Primus stoves, pots and pans—all things that the

Eskimo wanted in return for skins. He could have so many cans for a skin. A rifle might equal five skins or a bag of coffee a tenth of a skin. Gradually from his primitive system of barter a new currency had evolved. On the front counter was a "cash box" full of wooden bars, which, by their use as such, had come to be called "skins." I remembered a lecture of my father to his children on currency. Currency among other things should be durable; it should be portable. These wooden "skins" were much easier to handle than the fur ones, and undoubtedly an Eskimo could collect enough by trading furs to buy a stove, or possibly a tent for summer. For the Eskimos were becoming educated to the white man's scale of living.

"It's tough on them right now," one trader explained. "Bad times."

It was the summer of 1931. "Bad times" sounded very familiar. But that bad times should reach even Baker Lake, which seemed so isolated, so out of touch with the world, startled us.

"With bad times and Russian competition and the fox farms, the Eskimo can't get enough for his skins to live on white man's standards. It's pretty hard on him too, since he's got used to it."

We walked through to the back of the shop, a big barn of a room that smelled of dust, and animal, and that box in the cedar chest with your old fur neckpiece. A great loft on one side of the room piled with dark and light masses of fur looked softer and springier than a haymow. I tried to distinguish the different kinds of fur. There, tied together, was a bundle of white tails. There, you could see nothing but the crackly parchment side of skins. Rough caribou skins in another corner. (We saw caribou on the next flight, moving across the tundra like the shadow of a cloud.)

The trader climbed up a ladder to the loft. "Here," he said, taking something from a white pile, "there's a nice skin," throwing it down to me. White plumes falling through the dusty air. I caught it in my arms.

Strange that an animal should be reduced to this thing, light and ethereal as smoke, soft, luxurious, precious, the queen of furs—white fox. It was the white fox at Baker Lake that kept them all there. Lynn, if he could only get enough white fox, would go home next year. For they all looked forward to going home. Even those who were "bushed" saved their money for going *outside*.

Lynn would have to squint to see this animal in his trap on the snow. White against white. Only a shadow to tell there was something there—a shadow, and perhaps, on closer view, the black tip of a nose, the gray trap, and scarlet of torn flesh: a white fur collar for an evening coat!

It was very cold on the beach the last morning. "A tang of autumn in the air!" said one of the Hudson's Bay men. (It was the fourth of August.) The sky and lake were as gray as the day we landed. A cold wind ruffled some little yellow flowers below our feet, almost the only sign of growth beside the moss. We were waiting for the Eskimo family to assemble for a photograph. Our trader friends stood around. "Where's the Mounted?" we asked, looking at the group. "Oh, he's gone to get the old lady over in the camp there." Down the slope trooped the Eskimos; the little bright-eyed boys first, in knit caps and sweaters; the men in hoods; and then—"There she is!" In the tail of the procession came the "Mounted" in his red coat and brass buttons, and on his arm, a gallantly curved arm, hung the "old lady," the oldest Eskimo woman in camp. (Just like a wedding, I thought, the head usher leading the bride's mother—"the bride's mother wore . . .")

"May I present the old lady, Mrs. Lindbergh?" asked the "head usher," bowing to me. She looked a hundred years old, shriveled and almost bald, her brown face wrinkled as wrapping paper, her toothless mouth grinning and making funny little moans of joy. She had on a deerskin suit and trousers, and over her shoulders, as a cloak, hung, slightly awry, a ragged calico petticoat.

"May I present—" asked the "Mounted," bowing to me. The old lady giggled and so did I.

After the picture, my husband examined our plane, which was pulled up on the beach and anchored to fifty-gallon gasoline drums. These rusty barrels which had been sent up to Baker Lake to refuel one of the Northern expeditions stood about the beach, tipsily balanced in the heavy sand, like so many shipwrecked boats waiting to be reclaimed. I wondered if they would ever be taken out. It was hardly worth the lugging. Pulled up high on the gravelly part of the beach was a broken pair of pontoons which had brought some flier in to Baker Lake but never took him back. They were torn in the ice and, like discarded shoes, might lie there forever. I had a panicky feeling, as though I were watching the last train coast out of a lonely station at night, the lights twinkling into blackness down the track. How terrible to be left here, I thought, glancing at our orange-winged ship. It looked so tame and domesticated, tethered placidly to shore, like some barnyard animal. I could hardly believe that there was power and freedom in that smooth body, as life and death lie imprisoned in the shining shell of a bullet— that at a touch it would wake roaring and, once released, would rise easily as a bit of bark caught under a rock in a stream rises. But now, the engine asleep, the pontoons caught in the sand, the wings tied to shore, it looked as earth-bound as we. This was our one hope of escape. I turned to the *Sirius* and said with silent passion, "You *must* take us out."

One dark morning the following winter I was sitting at breakfast opening letters. A square fat one—nice paper—was in my hand. Invitation or advertisement? A printed leaflet—picture: a lady in ermine and fox waiting at the opera house for her limousine. "Revillon Frères—Private Showing."

"Revillon Frères." Baker Lake. The gray shore line. Guffaws of men. "Tickets for the show tonight!" "What's it like *outside?*" The neat white shack on the beach. The smell of that back room. The feathery pile in the loft. White plumes falling through the dusty air. I had my private showing in the summer.

SEVEN

Aklavik

❁

It was a quiet morning in the little river settlement, with only an occasional howl from a "husky" pulling at his chain. There was nothing to break the stillness of the glassy river at our feet, the stillness of that perfectly even skyline, wave following wave of pointed tips of pine trees. Life was going on as usual. Some Eskimo women padded by our bungalow, babies on their backs, their long ruffled calico skirts swinging gently to their gait.

Perhaps they were going to the Hudson's Bay store next door, perhaps to the Roman Catholic hospital beyond. It was baking day at the mission. The Eskimo schoolboys were down in the white-raftered kitchen mixing dough. The settlement's doctor had already finished his rounds at one of the two hospitals and was starting work at the second. (Both Catholics and Anglicans supported mission hospitals here.) The Anglican nurse had been up for hours, scrubbing floors, making beds, bathing patients and oiling babies. There were only two nurses to do everything in the hospital, from heavy cleaning to delicate surgical technique. The radio men up on the hill were at their schedules, touching Alaska and Canada with their quick fingers.

Suddenly a boy shouted and excitement spilled over

the camp. Scuffle of running feet—doors slamming—
screams of children. All the dogs began to howl. We
ran out of the bungalow. "The boat! The boat is coming
—look!—the smoke." There was no boat in sight; our
eyes followed the satin surface of the river until it disappeared around the next point. But looking beyond,
over the tops of the pine forest, one could see between
green points a small white plume, unmistakably foreign
to the landscape. The last boat of the year was slowly
making its way down the maze of streams of the
Mackenzie delta to Aklavik. It would take her hours
to reach the settlement. For though the whiff of smoke
did not look at any great distance, and a boat could
make good time downstream, she had still a long
journey. Only someone who had seen the river from
the air could appreciate how that silver ribbon would
lead a boat back and forth capriciously, like a child's
game of *follow the leader*, in and out, across a maze of
streams and woods until, with a sudden jerk around a
corner, it would land her at her own front door.

Our first sight of the Mackenzie delta was twelve
hours before. We had flown all night from Baker Lake.
It never grew dark. For hours I watched a motionless
sun set in a motionless cloud-bank. For hours we skirted
that gray, treeless coast, stretches on stretches of bleak
land scattered with icy lakes. Always the same. Until I
wondered, in spite of the vibration of the engine which
hummed up through the soles of my feet, whether we
were not motionless too. Were we caught, frozen into
some timeless eternity there in the North? The world
beneath had no reality that could be recognized, measured, and passed over. I knew that the white cloud-
bank out to sea hung over the ice pack—that it marked,
like the fiery ring around an enchanted castle, the outer
circle of a frozen kingdom we could not enter. I knew
from my husband's chart, handed back from time to
time, that we followed the shore of Canada along
Amundsen Gulf to the Beaufort Sea. At one time we

crossed a gray arm of coast which he pointed out as
a tip of Victoria Island. "Victoria Island"—one of those
pale pink lands which float off the top of the map—no,
I could not believe it.

In the middle of the night I tried to break the unreality by getting in touch with some radio station. It
was late, but Coppermine, a trading post a hundred
miles south, might be listening for us. I sent out our
position: "Over - - - Cape - - - Crocker - - - north - - - of
- - - Bathurst - - - inlet - - - 3:45 GCT (Greenwich civil
time) - - - Lindbergh." Would anyone believe us!
Recklessly, I even sent out a message on short wave to
the station at North Beach near New York. It was ten
forty-five in the evening in New York. No sound, no
reply to my message, but through the ear-phones I
could hear dimly some big station's unintelligible rattle.
Perhaps Edmonton—perhaps Chicago or New York.
Perhaps even, over the top of the world, Japan or
China. I sat back and closed my eyes to the gray wastes
below me, those fields of the moon. An exile on another
planet, I listened to the far-off chatter of the world.

Finally the sun set. Caught just below the horizon,
it continued to light the sky with a strange green glow,
like that from a partial eclipse. We turned our backs
on it and set our course southwest toward Aklavik. The
land stretched out dark ahead of us.

We were both quite sleepy as we turned this corner of the flight. My husband, who had done all the
flying, gave me the controls while he slept for short
periods of a few minutes. Then he would fly again
while I slept. During one of these naps I was jerked
awake. Splutter—putt, putt, putt. The engine stopped.
The nose of the ship dropped. We swayed forward. I
could see my husband bent over the gas valves. Then
the comforting splutter, splutter of the engine picking
up again. One of the pontoon tanks had run dry. That
was all. But I was stark awake by this time and wondering where we would land if the motor failed. I had
been flying by compass and by that indistinct line, like

the dregs of a wine bottle, that meant the horizon. Now I looked down at the ground below.

There, spread out for miles ahead, like so much tangled silver thread, were the meandering channels and watercourses worn by the Mackenzie River on the last slow lap of its journey to the Beaufort Sea. So many and so tortuous were the streams which made up this mammoth delta that I wondered how we would ever find the right bend in the right river, and Aklavik. Each circling stream had about the same course, the same number of tributary streams, some desultory and half choked with mud, others completely stopped at one end, making half-moon lakes—silver sickles of water.

As we came down lower and skimmed over the surface of one stream, we could not see across to another, for the banks were pine-covered. A strange sight in this treeless land, as though the great army of firs which had started out to accompany the Mackenzie River only a short distance had decided not to abandon her completely until she had safely reached the end of her journey, and had marched by her side even into this barren land, a thin phalanx of green.

It was three o'clock in the morning when we finally found the settlement—a big settlement for the North, about twenty or thirty houses, two churches, radio masts, and even another plane pulled up on the bank. At this hour it was so light that people ran out of their bungalows with cameras to take pictures.

As the roar of the motor died we heard for the first time that sound peculiar to the North, a bedlam of howling dogs. The term "howling dog" suggests back yards. This was the cry of a wild animal. And yet it was essentially the cry of resentment against the intruder—a strange bird which, roaring down the river, had broken the silence of their white night.

Today again there was intrusion from the outside world. The boat was coming in. The huskies, who had

started their protests early in the morning, continued
to howl as the small village turned out for its holiday.
By noon a leisurely procession had formed along the
path to the landing. A crowd of Eskimos: women in
their full calico skirts, men in pointed caps, little Eskimo
boys scuffing up the dust, all shy and smiling. Here was
a white-uniformed Canadian nurse from the hospital.

"Poor Kay," I heard behind me. "She's on duty and
won't be able to see it." It was a tragedy, I realized,
not to witness the docking of the boat.

There were the Mounted Police in their red coats,
standing head and shoulders above the crowd. The
three radio operators were speculating when the boat
would arrive.

Down the path from the mission school marched
a train of Eskimo children, the girls all wearing magenta
kerchiefs over their hair. They were shepherded by
two of the Gray Nuns of Montreal. The full gray
Mother Hubbard skirts of the sisters brushed the
ground. Poke bonnets hid their bright, smooth faces.
They looked delicate as the figures in old French prints,
far too delicate to survive the hard work in the North.
We found the next day, when we inspected the ram-
bling frame mission house, how well they had adapted
themselves to the life there. The Eskimo children in
the school were not only taught sewing and cooking,
dressmaking and shoe cobbling, gardening and
carpentry, but also fishing, fish cleaning and drying.
(The Eskimos feed their dogs and often themselves
largely on dried fish.) The French Canadian sister who
showed me the fish-drying shack rubbed her hands as
she shut the door on the stench, "Eet ees hard for us
to learrn—that!" It was more appropriate, I thought,
to have them making the paper chain decorations and
lanterns that were strung around the walls of the play
room. Lacy paper festoons and wreaths framed the
colored pictures of Christ. And in the boys' room,
hanging from the ceiling, was an old valentine, opening like an accordion to display a blue paper airplane

covered with forget-me-nots and roses and carrying Cupid. "The boys are so interest' een airplans," explained the sweet-faced sister.

But the boat was coming today. "Airplanes" were dreams, the boat was real. It came, like Christmas, only rarely and loaded with presents. Around the corner it chugged at last, pushing a big barge ahead. Tubby and white, like an old Hudson River excursion boat, its great wheels churned up a foamy wake. Everyone looked at the barge, which was loaded with freight—drums of gasoline, crates, boxes, sacks, and, in the midst of this cargo, a somewhat bedraggled team of huskies.

"Perhaps that big crate there is my engine." "Do you see our washtub?" Everyone speculated, like children on Christmas Eve catching first sight of mysterious packages. "Doesn't look like much gasoline—hope there's more inside," someone remarked. "I hope my shoes are there," cried a pretty girl. "Look at those huskies—lot of police in those dogs—don't look as strong as the others." "Perhaps mother sent me some fresh tomatoes."

At this moment, simultaneously with the boat whistle, there was a tremendous uproar. The dogs on shore had discovered their rivals on the barge. The intrusion of strange boats and planes and people was bad enough, but the intrusion of a strange pack of dogs meant war. For the time being they could only howl their protests, baring their fangs and panting at their chains. Had they been loose, they would have destroyed each other, fighting as they often do, team against team.

A moment of suspense before the boat was actually wedded to shore. Now it is still a boat, still a child of the water, and now, with the whipping of ropes, the clanking of chains, the long shudder as the gangplank is let down—now it is land.

A rush from the crowd to board her. "Wait—they're going to take the steer off first!" The steer came out of the jaws of the hold docilely enough at first, led by the ring in his nose, but finding himself alone in the middle of the gangplank, facing a noisy crowd and an arena of wild dogs, he balked and looked around imperiously, reminding me of the pictures of captive kings dragged in the triumphal processions of Roman conquerors. Then a yank from in front, a prod from behind, and he stepped off with infinite dignity.

"Now—we can get on! Look—Aggie's on the top deck already!" And the crowd swarmed up the gangplank, through the hold, up the stairs to the main cabin and the purser's office, where a line formed waiting for letters, packages, and news of freight. Those who had already found their belongings wandered about the decks and saloons, thinking perhaps of the last time they were there, on the trip up to their new home, from Edmonton or some point in southern Canada. The boat then had seemed such a self-sufficient world. Here one walked; here one sat; here one ate. Nothing outside mattered. The windows, the walls of the ship, were bulwarks shutting out anything beyond. Mud banks, pine trees, settlements, slipped by without scratching through to one's consciousness. They were unreal picture-post card slides. But today, sitting in the ship's saloon, looking out to the shores of a new home, one saw that it was the boat which became unreal. Against the looming importance of the new life it began to shrink. In front of the vivid, crowded bank it became colorless and transparent. The boat was no longer impregnable. Aklavik with a flood of fresh associations and meanings broke in through the doors and windows, poured down the portholes, spilled over the deck, divesting the boat of any life of its own. One might well look around in amazement, seeing it now for what it had always been, a thin shell through which the sea of life pounded endlessly.

It was evening in the river camp. The backwash from the morning's excitement had rippled out into yards and front porches. Half-opened crates and boxes, broken slats of wood, wrapping paper, excelsior, and cardboard cartons lay scattered in front of the bungalows. Small groups of people stood around each pile examining the spoils of the day.

"That's the new tank for our motor boat." The doctor, a hammer in his hand, bent over a half-open crate. "Why! They've sent the wrong kind—look here, Jennie—they've sent the wrong kind. And I wrote them all the specifications—can't use it—have to wait till next year." Suppose one had to wait a year for a new part for a car! And this tank was far more necessary. Its importance could be measured in lives. The doctor wanted it for the speed boat that was his fastest means of transportation in the summer. He had to cover a radius of several hundred miles, summer and winter, by boat and by dog team, in his care of the sick. Pulling teeth, delivering babies, operating for appendicitis, and treating tuberculosis were all in the day's work. His larger boat, *The Medico,* was fitted out as a hospital, operating room included. With this he went on longer trips to outlying spots once a year. Eskimos had to "save up" all their illnesses for the doctor's yearly visit. With the speed boat he could reach emergency cases much faster, but he had hardly any range because of the small gasoline tank.

"Now with a new tank—I had hoped—" He put down his hammer in discouragement. "But you see they've sent the wrong kind."

Two of the radio men went by with a crate on their shoulders. "We've got a bathtub," one of them shouted back. "You won't be able to lord it over us any more— a regular bathtub!" Heretofore the doctor had the settlement's only bathtub, an unporcelained tin one, filled from a teakettle.

Inside the bungalow the doctor's wife had a table piled with presents, a huge keg of orangeade, candy and cookies, fruit and vegetables and magazines. They looked so lovely there, lighting up the whole room, she couldn't put them away just yet.

Next door I saw a young wife tearing the wrappings off a baby's bathtub, carelessly leaving the huge carton, marked with cherubs and storks, in the front yard. After all, the neighbors would have to know sooner or later.

Down at the mission school newly baked loaves were piled high in the kitchen. The children were singing in a strange high chant the songs of the Sisters: "Wail-come . . . Wail-come . . . We wail-come you today."

The nurse at the hospital looked out for a moment at the now deserted river boat hugging the shore. The boat that had brought her here, she thought with a wave of homesickness. Perhaps she would be able to get off for an hour after supper. She had been too rushed all day.

A husky howled from the bank, the last retort of a long day's argument. An answering yelp from the opposite camp. Then silence.

EIGHT

Point Barrow

❁

"Dit-darr-darr, darr-dit-dit-darr, darr-dit-dit-dit." "WXB - - - WXB - - - WXB - - - de (from) - - - KHAL." The blurred buzz of my own radio-sending rang in my ears. Through the cockpit cover I could see fog on the water ahead, motionless piles of light gray cotton wool with dark gray patches here and there. Out to sea the white wall of fog stood impassable and still as the ice

packs from which it rose. Inland under floating islands
of fog stretched the barren Arctic land. We were turning toward it as our only chance of reaching Point Barrow, the bleak northern tip of Alaska. Could we get
through that night? If the weather ahead was not
worse. I must get my message to the Barrow operator.

"wxb - - - wxb - - - wxb," I called to him.

"Dit-darr-dit!" A sharp clean note came through
my receiver. There he was! Right on the watch, though
I had called him off schedule. Then there really was a
man waiting for us, I thought with relief. There really
was a Point Barrow. We weren't jumping off into space.
Somewhere ahead in that white wilderness a man was
listening for us, guiding us in.

Now, my message: "Flying - - - thru - - - fog - - -
and - - - rain - - - going - - - inland - - - wea (weather)
- - - pse (please)?"

His notes came back clearly. I wrote rapidly not to
miss a word, "Low - - - fog - - - bank - - - rolling - - -
off - - - ice - - - now - - - clear - - - over - - - fog - - - expected - - - soon - - - pass - - - ground - - - vis (visibility) - - - one - - - mile." I poked the pad forward to my
husband in the front cockpit. He glanced at it and nodded. That meant "Ok. That's what I wanted to know.
We'll push on."

On for hours through the unreal shifting world of
soft mist. Here a cloud and there a drizzle; here a wall
and there, fast melting, a hole through which gleamed
the hard metallic scales of the sea. That was no mirage.
That rippling steel below us was real. If one flew into
it blindly it might as well be steel. At times we seemed
to be riding on its scaly back and then, with a roar, up
we climbed into white blankness. No sight of land; no
sight of sea or sky; only our instruments to show the
position of the plane. Circling down again, my husband
motioned me to reel in the antenna. We were flying
too near the water. The ball-weight on the end might
be snapped off. Perhaps we might even be forced to

land unexpectedly on open sea and have both weight
and wire torn off at the impact. His gesture was a danger signal for me and I waited, tense, for the nod and
second gesture, "All right now—reel out again." At
times we would come out of the fog, not into daylight
but into the strange gray night. The Arctic sun just
under the horizon still lit the sky with a light that did
not belong to dawn or dusk. A cold gray light that
seemed to grow off the ice pack.

We should be very near by now. Would we be able
to get through or would we have to turn back? The
fog was closing in behind us. It might be impossible to
return to Aklavik. A note from the front cockpit—
"Weather at Barrow?" We were flying under the fog
again, too low to trail a long antenna. I reeled out a few
feet of wire, which would not allow me to transmit
messages but was sufficient for receiving. It all
depended on the man at Barrow. If only he would go
on sending in spite of our silence. We were powerless
to let him know.

"Weather, weather, *weather*—send us weather," I
pleaded mentally and put on my ear-phones. Silence.
Wisps of fog scudded past us. No, there he was, "Darr-
dit-darr, dit-dit-dit-dit," calling us. Twice, three times,
four times—then silence again, waiting for us to answer. I held my breath, "Weather, weather." There
he goes again. "Do - - - u (you) - - - hear - - - me?"
came the message. Silence again. He was waiting for
my call. "Yes, yes," I answered silently, "but I can't
send—go ahead—*weather!*"

"Darr-dit-darr; dit-dit-dit-dit." There he was again.
My pencil took down the letters, slowly spelling out the
message, "Fog - - - lifting - - - fast (Good man! He did
it!) - - - visibility - - - two - - - miles (He did it! Good
for him!) don't - - - think - - - u - - - have - - - any - - -
trouble - - - find - - - lagoon." There it was—just what
we wanted. I poked my husband excitedly with the
pad. That operator at Barrow—he did it—we'd get

through all right now. "Fog lifting, visibility two miles."
Oh, what a grand man!

We could see the gray flat coast line now and
watched it closely for Barrow. That might be it—a
stretch of whitish irregular blocks—houses? No, as we
came nearer, they were the strange pushed-up blocks
of the ice pack crushed against a little harbor. Well,
these were houses. We had come on a small low spit
of land squeezed between two seas of ice blocks. Yes,
there were houses. We peered down at them eagerly,
four tipsy weather-beaten shacks and a few tents, the
color of the ice blocks. Can this be Barrow? I almost
cried with disappointment looking at that deserted
group. No sign of a person, no sign of smoke, no sign of
life. It *can't* be Barrow. Childishly, my first thought
ran on, "Why, that radio man said they'd have a regular
Thanksgiving dinner for us. There couldn't be any
dinner down there—no smoke." I felt very hungry. We
circled again. "No!" I realized with relief. "No radio
mast! It isn't Barrow." We followed the shore line until we found a larger and newer group of houses between the ice pack and an open lagoon. This was Barrow, ten or twelve red roofs, numerous shacks and
tents, a church steeple and—yes, there they were—the
radio masts.

We were landing on the lagoon. I pulled off two
bulky pairs of flying socks and put on a pair of rubber-
soled shoes for walking. Although it was not freezing
weather, my feet became numb before we reached
the small crowd of people on shore. A strange group
huddled together in the half-light of the Arctic night.
I looked at them—pointed hoods, fur parkas, sealskin
boots—and thought at first, "They're *all* Eskimos." No,
that must be the radio man in the khaki mackinaw. I
felt a glow of gratitude and waved at him. As we
climbed up the bank the crowd of Eskimos drew back,
an attitude of respect and wonder never seen in the
usual crowd. As they moved a great cry arose—not a

shout, but a slow deep cry of welcome. Something in it akin to the bleak land and the ice pack.

Then, after shaking of hands and a confusion of voices, I found myself running across the icy moss toward a lighted frame house. My hostess, the doctor's wife, was leading me. I stamped my numb feet on the wooden steps of her home as she pushed open the door. The warmth of a kitchen fire, the brightness of gas lamps, and a delicious smell of sweet potatoes and freshly baked muffins poured out around me and drew me in.

A long table spread for our "Thanksgiving dinner" filled the living room. White cloth, rims of plates, curves of spoons, caught the light from swinging lamps above. I looked around quickly and felt the flavor of an American home—chintz curtains drawn aside, pictures of "woodland scenes" on the walls, bright pillows on the sofa, and there, in the window, a box of climbing nasturtiums.

In the other south window I noticed a tomato plant bent under the weight of one green tomato. My hostess smiled, "That tomato won't ever ripen, you know—it hasn't enough sun—but the leaves grow and we can smell it. Even the smell of growing vegetables is good to us." I looked outside at the pale gray moss on the ground. "I didn't use the dirt around here," she went on to explain. "I tried to, at first, but it's really nothing but frozen sand. Nothing will grow in it except that moss. I carried this earth in a box all the way from Nome."

No vegetables! I tried to realize what she was explaining to me. All their provisions came in by boat once a year around the tip of Alaska from the little mining town, Nome. There was only a month or two in the summer when the icy waters were clear enough for a boat to reach Barrow, and even then the ice pack, jammed against the shore for weeks at a time, might make it impossible. This year their boat, the *Northland*, also carrying our fuel supply, was waiting a hundred

miles down the coast for a change in wind to blow the
ice pack offshore. "The schoolteacher and his wife are
waiting for their daughter. She is on that ship."

The settlement "family" began to crowd in, piling
their parkas and sealskin boots at the door of the warm
room. Every member had a vital part in the life of the
settlement.

The doctor and minister, our host, was leader of the
community. He had built the manse in which we were
staying. His son, "outside," had helped him to plan it.
The doctor himself, directing the Eskimos, had measured and fitted every board and nail. He had placed
special insulation in the floor, for it was impossible to
have a furnace in the cellar. If you started to thaw out
the ground underneath, the house might sink. And a
furnace would require too much fuel in a fuel-less
country. The windows, triple storm ones, were all
nailed down. They were for light and not for ventila-
tion. Windows that open and shut are always draughty.
The rooms were ventilated by pipes which let in air
indirectly but kept out rain and snow. Heat from the
kitchen went up through ventilators in the ceiling to
the bedrooms above. There were big stoves in all the
rooms. The doctor installed the water tank, connected
it with pipes for running water downstairs, and heated
it from the stove. Aside from his work as architect and
carpenter, he preached every Sunday, had a Bible class
Wednesday nights, was doctor, surgeon, and dentist,
and was preparing his boy for college.

His wife and another trained nurse had supervision
of the hospital. The winter before there had been an
epidemic of diphtheria in the settlement. The little
hospital was crowded past its capacity but they had
managed all the work with only the help of a few un-
trained Eskimo girls.

The schoolteacher and his wife carried on their work
in a frame building heated only by a stove. One of the
Eskimo girls, sent from the Point Barrow School to
college at Sitka, had come back to teach this year. The

radio operator kept the community in touch with the outside world. Radio was their only means of communication except for the yearly boat and a few dog-team mails during the winter. He was responsible, too, for keeping the world in touch with them, sending meteorologists daily reports of the important Arctic weather. His wife was bringing up, besides a girl of nine, a six-month-old baby named Barrow.

An old Scotch whaleman completed the circle as we sat at dinner. He had not been "outside" for forty years, had never seen telephones or automobiles, although radio had come to take a regular part in his life and airplanes had landed near his home several times. The Wilkins Polar Expedition had based at Barrow and a plane carrying serum had flown up the year before in the diphtheria epidemic. It was strange to realize that radio and aviation, which typify the latest advance in civilization, had vitally affected this outpost, while railroad, telephone, and telegraph had not touched it.

We sat down to a real Thanksgiving dinner. Provisions were short but they had all pooled their supplies for a feast. Reindeer meat came out of the community cellar, a huge cave dug down in the icy ground. The radio operator carved a wild goose that had been shot near by. Among their remaining cans of food they had found sweet potatoes, peas, and beets. There was even a salad of canned celery and fruit. Someone still had a few eggs (not fresh, of course; preserved ones), which were brought over for mayonnaise. Someone else had flour for the soda biscuits. Someone brought coffee. But the greatest treat of the evening, the most extravagant, generous touch, I did not properly appreciate. The trained nurse had grown a little parsley in the hospital window box. They had picked it to put around the platter of meat. I treated it as garniture.

On Sunday the whole Eskimo village came up the hill to the white frame church. Men in their fur jackets

and big sealskin boots; women with babies on their
backs under their loose fur-lined calico dresses; little
children with bright slit eyes shining out of fur hoods—
all padded up the hill out of their tents and shacks.
Sunday service was a great occasion and they were all
smiling and laughing. No one wanted to miss it. I looked
for the Eskimo friends I had made in the last two or
three days. "Lottie," who led us over the ice pack the
day before. When she ran she heaved from one side
to another like a bear. I could see her green calico
dress swaying in the crowd. "Ned" and his wife, who
made us a fur cap and mittens. "Bert," who kept the
village store and supervised the killing of the reindeer
for the winter stock. We met him the day of the round-
up, sledging back carcasses, cleaned and tied up in
cheesecloth. Here were the Eskimo girls who helped
with the Thanksgiving dinner, shy and smiling, their
black hair brushed down sleekly; and the Eskimo
woman who gave us a miniature whaling spear carved
out of walrus tusk. They all crowded in between the
wooden benches of the church. During the service
there was a general shuffling and crying of babies.
Whenever a baby cried too much, the mother would
get up reluctantly, hitch her bundle higher up on her
back, and pad out clumsily. But nothing distracted the
congregation. Men, women, and children leaned forward earnestly watching the minister. Many could not
understand English. Even those who had learned it
in school were bewildered by psalms sung by a shep-
herd on a sun-parched hillside.

"'We have gone astray like sheep,'" began the
reading. Sheep, what did that mean to them? I saw
stony New England pastures and those gray backs moving among blueberry bushes and junipers.

"Like the reindeer," explained the minister, "who
have scattered on the tundras." The listening heads
moved. They understood reindeer.

"'Your garners will be filled.'" Big red barns, I saw,
and hay wagons rumbling uphill. But the Eskimos?

"Your meat cellars," the minister answered my question "will be full of reindeer meat."

" *'Your oxen will be strong,'* " read the next verse. "Your dogs for your dog teams will pull hard," continued the minister. " *'The Power of God.'* " How could he explain that abstract word *Power?*

"Sometimes when the men are whaling," he started, "the boats get caught in the ice. We have to take dynamite and break up the ice to let them get out. That is power—dynamite—'the dynamite of God.' "

"For Thine is the Kingdom, 'the dynamite,' and the Glory forever and ever. Amen," I said over to myself.

The congregation was standing up to sing. The schoolteacher's small boy, who was organist, sounded the chords. "Glor*ee* for me— Glor*ee* for me." A buoyant hymn generally, but sung by these people in a high singsong chant, it held a minor quality of endlessness, as though it might echo on and on over the gray tundras—"that would be glor*ee*, glor*ee* for me."

One morning we woke to find the weather changed. The sun was a pale moon behind the scattering mist. "Have you arranged your radio schedule?" my husband asked me. "We ought to leave." I ran down the boardwalk that covered the wet moss to the government radio shack.

The weather had not changed enough for them. Everyone was watching the manse flagpole. "Still northwest," the flag read. The ice pack still hugged the shore line, blocking their boat, the *Northland,* off Icy Cape. "Perhaps you will fly over it!" "You can signal to them anyway!" "When you get 'outside,' perhaps you will read somewhere in the papers whether or not our boat got in. It usually has, but when it doesn't—" They were all standing around us saying good-by. "We have no more butter left." "Or flour." "Or tea or coffee." "I would like a package of cigarettes," admitted the radio operator with a smile. A package of cigarettes! If only we had thought to bring a few things like that. Our heavily loaded plane could not have carried much food, but a package of cigarettes, a newspaper, some fresh fruit—I longed to have something to give them. At least we could carry out letters and messages. Someone had a daughter in China and we were going—they could hardly believe it—to China.

"Good-by! Good-by! We'll see you again." Perhaps the veteran whaleman would never face the blast of motor horns and the jangle of street cars but some of the others might leave Barrow. The doctor's son was coming back to college. One of the young Eskimo men was hopefully taking a correspondence course in aviation. Poor man, he was waiting at that moment for the *Northland* to bring in his home work for the next year.

We started to put on our heavy flying clothes. Over two pairs of heavy double-weight socks I pulled on the boots they had given me. Made of sealskin, sewed and chewed into shape by the Eskimo women, they were the warmest, dryest, lightest shoes I have ever worn. My husband drew on his flying suit. His knee hit against a lump in the pocket—an orange they had given us as we left Churchill a week before! "Perhaps you'd like this," he said, half apologetically, handing it to the doctor's wife.

"An orange!" She held it in her palms for a moment as though warming her hands by its glow and then said, with the enthusiasm of a girl spending a birthday coin, "I'll tell you what we'll do! We'll give it to the baby! Wonderful—for Barrow!"

NINE

Dark

❁

"What time does it get dark at Nome?" My husband pushed a penciled message back to me. Dark? I had completely forgotten that it ever was dark. We had been flying in the land of the midnight sun, though actually its period was over in August. The sun set, but the sky did not darken on either of the flights, from Baker Lake to Aklavik, or from Aklavik to Barrow. But tonight—for it was about eight-thirty in the evening—the light was fading rather fast. Streaks of the remaining sunset ran gold in the inlets and lagoons of the coast. We had turned the corner of Alaska after leaving Point Barrow and were flying south to the little mining town, Nome, on the Bering coast. An unknown route, an unknown harbor; we must have light to land.

"WXB - - - WXB - - - WXB," I called back to our friend at the Barrow radio station. I had tried in vain to reach Nome. "Nil - - - hrd (nothing heard) - - - from - - - WXY (Nome) - - - or - - - WXW (Kotzebue) - - - what - - - time - - - does - - - it - - - get - - - dark - - - at - - - Nome?" His faint signals traced dim incomprehensible marks on my brain, then faded away. It was no use; I could not make them out. I would have to let go of that thread and pick up another.

"Can't - - - copy - - - ur (your) - - - sigs (signals) - - - will - - - contact - - - NRUL (the *Northland*)." I signed off. There was no time to lose. Again I tried, "NRUL - - - de - - - KHCAL - - - nil - - - hrd - - - from - - - WXY - - - what - - - time - - - does - - - it - - - get - - - dark - - - at - - - Nome?" No answer. The sparks from the exhaust flashed behind us in the growing dusk.

Was it really going to get dark? It had not been dark since Baker Lake, since that evening when we set out recklessly at seven to fly all night. It had seemed, I remembered, a kind of madness to start at that hour. It would soon be dark, or so I thought, and to fly at night, in a strange country, through uncertain weather to an unknown destination—what were we thinking of! Spendthrifts with daylight, we who usually counted every coin; who always rose early to fly, at three or four in the morning, not to waste a second of the precious light; we were down at the field, the engine warmed up and ready to start with the first streaks of dawn, in order "to get there by dark." Dark—that curfew hour in a flier's mind, when the gates are closed, the portcullis dropped down, and there is no way to go around or to squeeze under the bars if one is late.

But that night at Baker Lake, we were going north, into the land of the midnight sun.

"And it will be light all the way?" we had asked incredulously. (Though of course we knew it to be so.)

"Sure—it won't get dark at all—going north like that." The game warden had nodded his head. "Light all the way!"

Going into that strange world of unending day was like stepping very quietly across the invisible border of the land of Faery that the Irish poets write of, that timeless world of Fionn and Saeve, or the world of Thomas the Rhymer. It was evening when we left Baker Lake, but an evening that would never flower into night, never grow any older. And so we had set out, released from fear, intoxicated with a new sense of freedom—out into that clear unbounded sea of day. We could go on and on and never reach the shores of night. The sun would set, darkness would gather in the bare coves, creep over the waste lands behind us, but never overtake us. The wave of night would draw itself together, would rise behind us and never break.

But now—going south— My husband switched on the instrument lights. We were running short of fuel. Our gasoline barrels were on the icebound *Northland*

and we had not refueled since Aklavik. There was no chance of turning back. We must land before dark.

"NRUL - - - NRUL - - - what - - - time - - - does - - - it - - - get - - - dark - - - at - - - Nome?"

At Barrow, I remembered, we had even wanted the dark. When I went to bed the first night, I had pulled down the shades, trying to create the feeling of a deep black night. For sleep, one needs endless depths of blackness to sink into; daylight is too shallow, it will not cover one. At Aklavik, too, I had missed night's punctuality. It was light when we went to bed and light when we rose. The same light shed over breakfast and lunch and supper and continued on through bedtime, so that I hardly knew when to feel tired or when to feel hungry.

But now, seeing signs of approaching night—the coves and lagoons took up the light the sky was losing —I was afraid. I felt the terror of a savage seeing a first eclipse, or even as if I had never known night. What was it? Explorer from another planet, I watched with fear, with amazement, and with curiosity, as Emily Dickinson watched for day:

> Will there really be a morning?
> Is there such a thing as day?
> Could I see it from the mountains
> If I were as tall as they?
>
> Has it feet like water-lilies?
> Has it feathers like a bird?
> Is it brought from famous countries
> Of which I have never heard? [1]

"Feathers like a bird," perhaps, answered my own questioning. The shadow of a wing covered all the sky.

[1] From *The Poems of Emily Dickinson*, Centenary Edition. Edited by Martha Dickinson Bianchi and Alfred Leete Hampson. Reprinted by permission of Little, Brown & Company.

We would be covered, inclosed, crushed. Wisps of evening fog below grew luminous in the approaching dark. I remembered now what night was. It was being blind and lost and trapped. It was looking and not seeing—that was night.

"wxy - - - wxy - - - wxy - - - what - - - time - - - does - - - it - - - get - - - dark - - - at - - - Nome?"

Suddenly an answer: wxn - - - wxn - - - Candle - - - Candle—" One of the relay stations on the coast had heard us, "Will - - - stand - - - by - - - in - - - case - - - you - - - don't - - - get - - - wxy," came their message. At last someone to answer.

"What - - - time - - - does - - - it - - - get - - - dark - - - at - - - Nome?"

There was a silence while he relayed the message to Nome. I looked out and caught my breath. The sea and sky had merged. The dark had leaped up several steps behind me when my back was turned. I would have to keep my eye on him or he would sneak up like the child's game of steps. But the radio was buzzing. My head went down again.

"The - - - men - - - are - - - going - - - to - - - put - - - flares - - - on - - - Nome - - - River," came back the answer, "it's - - - overcast - - - and - - - getting - - - dark." Then, continuing, "When - - - u (you) - - - expect - - - arrive - - - so - - - they - - - no (know) - - - when - - - lite - - - flares?"

I passed my scribbled message forward. The lights blinked on in the front cockpit. I read by my own light the reply, "Arrive in about 1½ hours—don't lite flares until plane circles and blinks lites."

An hour and a half more! It would be night when we landed! Turned inland, we were over the mountains now and there were peaks ahead. It was darker over the land than over the water. Valleys hoard darkness as coves hoard light. Reservoirs of darkness, all through the long day they guard what is left them from the night before; but now their cups were filling up, trembling at the brim, ready to spill over. The wave of night climbed up behind us; gathering strength from every crevice, it towered over us.

Suddenly my husband pulled the plane up into a stall, throttled the engine, and, in the stillness that followed, shouted back to me, "Tell him there's fog on the mountains ahead. We'll land for the night and come into Nome in the morning."

"All right, where are we?"

"Don't know exactly—northwest coast of Seward Peninsula."

Without switching on the light I started tapping rapidly, "wxn - - - wxn - - - wxn - - - fog - - - on - - - mountains - - - ahead - - - will - - - land - - - for - - - night - - - and - - - come - - - into - - - Nome - - - morning - - - position - - - northwest - - - - coast - - - Seward - - - Peninsula," I repeated twice.

"Hurry up! Going to land," came a shout from the front cockpit. We were banking steeply.

No time to try again. No time to listen for reply. I did not know if they had received it, but we could not wait to circle again. We must land before that last thread of light had gone.

Down, down, down, the cold air whistling through the cowlings as we dived toward the lagoon. I must wind in the antenna before we hit the water. The muscles in my arms stiffened to soreness turning the wheel at top speed, as though I were reeling in a gigantic fish from the bottom of the sea. One more turn—*jiggle, snap,* the ball-weight clicked into place—all wound up, safe. Now—brace yourself for the landing. How *can* he see anything! Spank, spank, spank. There we go—I guess we're all right! But the ship shot on through the water—on and on. Must have landed "down wind." Now it eased up a little. There, I sighed with relief. We were taxiing toward that dark indistinct line ahead—a shore. About half a mile off my husband pulled back the throttle, idled the engine for a few seconds, then cut the switch. In the complete stillness that followed, he climbed out on to the pontoon.

"Think we'd better anchor here." He uncoiled the rope and threw out our anchor. Splash! There it stayed under about three feet of water with the rope floating on top. Heavens! Pretty shallow—thought we had more room than that. Well, we were anchored anyway. We were down—we were safe. Somewhere out on the wild coast of Seward Peninsula.

At Nome it was dark now. The bonfire that was to have welcomed us lit up an empty shore as the crowd straggled home. It was dark where we were on the coast of Seward Peninsula. A little light surprised us from the blackness miles away—a single Eskimo camp perhaps. We made a bed in the baggage compartment out of our parachutes, our flying suits, and sleeping bag, and stretched out. The wave of night broke over us and we slept.

We slept—but not for long. I had only time to turn over twice—fly around the world, run from savages, drop pebbles in the Black Sea, paint the corners of the Mediterranean a deeper blue with a very long paint brush—when—*putt, putt, putt*—something broke into the Mediterranean and my sleep. *Putt, putt, putt*—I wasn't in the Mediterranean. I was nowhere. I was in Alaska, on a lagoon, far off from civilization, where perhaps no white man had been before. *Putt, putt, putt.* Were those voices?

"Hul-lo!"

"Charles! What's that!"

We both woke with a terrible start. My husband crawled aft, pushed back the sliding hatch and looked out. (The savages! I thought—they've come back again!)

"Hello," said my husband tentatively. Two small boats, both roofed with skins, were alongside our pontoons. In the cavelike mouth of one, a lantern lit up a circle of dark faces.

"Hul-lo!" I heard the same guttural voice hesitating with the words. "We—hunt—duck."

"Oh," said my husband, a little bewildered. "That's nice." (We were not in the wilds of Alaska after all.)

"You—land—here?" came the voice from the cave.

"Yes," answered my husband, "we came for the night." (Smiling.) "Do you see many of these around here?"

"Yes—yes—" said the man vaguely, not understanding at all.

"Get many ducks?" (What was one to make conversation about at three-thirty in the morning on the northwest coast of Seward Peninsula!)

"Well, guess I'll go back to bed." My husband closed the hatch and the boats disappeared.

To sleep again, but I could not get back to the Mediterranean.

TEN

The King Islanders

❁

ESKIMO SPORTS

Tomorrow Afternoon at 4 P.M.

At Barracks Sq. and Water Front

ESKIMO "WOLF DANCE" IN COSTUME

At Arctic Brotherhood Hall 8 P.M.

Public Invited

LINDBERGHS' BE GUESTS OF HONOR

The Nugget, Nome's daily telegraph bulletin, lay on the table, its front page announcing the day's entertainment. We had arrived in this old Alaskan mining town after a short flight from Shishmaref Inlet. The night mists had melted when we woke the morning after our adventure with the duck hunters. In front of us glistened a promised land. This was the Alaska we had read of. Snow-capped mountains climbed ahead of us instead of flat wastes. Green valleys cut the morning light. And the sea, the Bering Sea, rising in the gap between two hills as we approached, burned brilliant blue. We followed the beach, a gleaming white line, toward Safety Harbor. A second white line ran parallel to the shore, like foam or scattered flowers. As we came nearer I saw it to be a tangled trail of driftwood, polished white by the surf after its long journey down the Yukon River, out into Norton Sound, and up the coast to Nome. Pounding, dancing, tossing, all the way they had come, these white arms, these branches from an alien forest, to flower on a bare coast that had never known a tree. They were as startling to see here as the waxen stems of Indian pipe in the heart of green woods, ghostly visitors from another world.

No trees yet. We had come far south from Barrow, but there were still no trees on these green hills falling to the water's edge. A broad trail cut its way over the slope, rippling up and down, like a whip cracking in the air. An Eskimo trail, I supposed, until I saw a black beetle crawl around the corner. A car! A road! We had not seen a road for so long that I hardly recognized one.

A little later we were bumping along the same road on our way into town. It had been a trail in the Gold Rush days. Old roadhouses were stationed along the side, a day's dog-team journey apart over winter snow; we had already passed the second one in forty minutes. Dilapidated shingled buildings they were, fast becoming useless; for the airplane on skiis is replacing the dog team. It is cheaper per pound to fly.

Nome has changed since the Gold Rush days when

in the 1890's the precious metal was discovered in creeks and on the coast, and the great trail of prospectors swarmed over the mountains to that far cape of Alaska; when all the beach for miles—that white line we had seen from the air—was black with men sifting gold from the sand; when banks, hotels, theaters, and shops sprang up overnight and busy crowds thronged up and down the plank streets. Twenty thousand people once filled the town; now there are hardly more than a thousand.

But there were still signs of the old life. We passed a deserted mining shack by a stream. Fireweed, yarrow, and monkshood sprawled over the rusted machinery. On the beach two men were shoveling sand down long wooden sluice boxes, "washing" gold.

"Just about manage a day's wage that way," explained our host as we passed. Ahead was a gold dredge in action; the water pipes or "points" plunged deep into the ground to thaw it out before dredging.

The banks, the hotels, the shops, were still there as we rattled over the plank streets of Nome. Empty shells of buildings, many of them, gray, weather-beaten, sagging like an old stage set, tattered banners of a better day. But Nome was still busy. Besides a number of stores selling drugs and provisions, there were little shops showing moccasins and ivory work. One large window was a mass of climbing nasturtiums grown from a window box. There were boats coming in, trade and tourists. There was the loading and unloading of lighters in the harbor. That was what brought the King Islanders.

This Eskimo tribe from King Island in the north came to Nome in the summer to get what work they could as longshoremen and, perhaps, selling trinkets to tourists. They paddled eighty miles down the coast in huge "umiaks," walrus-skin boats holding twenty-five or thirty people. When they put to shore they tipped their boats upside down and made tents of them. Here under a curved roof they sat—those of the tribe who were not working in the harbor—and filed away at walrus-tusk ivory, making bracelets and cigarette holders.

Not today though. Today they were all down at the wharf, as we were, to see their Chief win the kyak race. For, of course, he would win. That was why he was Chief. He was taller and stronger and stood better and danced better and hunted better than anyone else in the tribe. When he ceased to excel, he would cease to be Chief. I wondered, looking at him, if he had to be browner than the rest of them, too. He stood quite near us on the dock, shaking his head and sturdy shoulders into a kind of raincoat, a hooded parka made of the gut of seals. His head emerging from the opening showed a streak of white across the dark crop of hair, and, looking at his face, one was shocked to see the same splash of white on the side of brow and cheek, as though the usual Eskimo brown were rubbing off. It was not a birthmark, they told me, but some strange disease which was slowly changing the color of his skin. Would it detract from his superiority or increase it? He seemed quite invincible as he stood there, his broad shoulders thrown back, his head well set. Even his features were stronger than those of his men; firmer mouth, more pronounced cheekbones, unusually deep-set eyes. He belonged to those born rulers of the earth.

The three men who were to race squeezed into their kyaks (a native boat entirely sealskin-covered except for a hole where the man sits). Each one then tied the skirt of his parka around the wooden rim of the opening so that no water could enter. Man and boat were one, like Greek centaurs. Then they were launched. A cold rain was driving in our faces and the bay was choppy, but the three kyaks, far more delicately balanced than canoes, rode through the waves like porpoises. It was difficult to follow the race. Sometimes the waves hid a boat from view, or breaking over one, covered it with spray. But the Chief won, of course. The crowd on the beach shouted. He did not come in; merely shook the water from his face and started to turn his kyak over in a side somersault. A little flip with the paddle and he was upside down. "That's how easily they turn over," I thought. For one horrible second the boat bobbed there in the surf, bottom up, like one of those annoying come-back toys with the weight stuck in the wrong end. A gasp from the crowd. Then, "A-a-ah!" everyone sighed with relief. He flipped right side up, smiled, shook the water off his face. What was he thinking as he shoved in to shore after that triumph? He had won. He had turned a complete somersault in rough water. No one else could do it as well. He was Chief of the King Islanders.

We saw him again at night. The bare raftered hall was jammed with the Eskimo and white inhabitants of Nome. Around the walls, as in an old-fashioned dancing school, sat a row of Eskimo mothers. Leaning over their calico skirts they peered at the audience and at the same time kept watch of their black-eyed children who sprawled in and out among the slat chairs. There was much giggling and rustling of paper programs. As the curtain rose one noticed first the back wall hung with furs, one huge white bearskin in the center. The stage itself was empty except for a long box, like a large birdhouse, in which were five portholes. On top of the box over each hole squatted an Eskimo in everyday dress: skin trousers, boots, and parka. Out of the holes suddenly popped five wolves' heads. Ears erect, fangs bared, yellow eyes gleaming, the heads nodded at us. Nodded, nodded, nodded, insanely like a dream, this way and that, to the rhythmic beat of a drum. For now in the background of the stage sat some Eskimo women and a few old men chanting and pounding out the rhythm of those heads. Every little while when a head became awry, the Eskimo on top leaned over and jerked it straight by pulling at an ear. The snarling heads began to look childish. Weren't those squatting figures just like the nurses in Central Park? "Tony! Anne! Christopher! come here—what have you done

to your coat? Look where your hat is! There now—go
along." They apparently had no part in the drama,
these nurses. Like the black-hooded figures who run in
and out on the Japanese stage, they were, I assumed,
supposed to be invisible, and only there for convenience.

Pound, pound, pound—out of the holes leaped the
wolves (who were dressed in long white woolen underwear below their fierce heads). On all fours they
stared at us. Pound, pound, pound—they nodded this
way, that way, this way, that way, unceasingly, like a
child who is entranced with a new trick and cannot
shake himself free of it, but repeats it again and again,
a refrain to his life. Pound, pound, pound—they were
on their feet and shaking their bangled gauntlets this
way and that. The wolf in the center tossed his head
and glared at us—the Chief of the King Islanders.
Pound, pound, pound, the nodding went on and on.
Pound, pound, pound, their movements were sudden
and elastic, like animals. There was more repose in their
movement than in their stillness, which was that of a
crouching panther, or a taut bow. One waited, tense,
for the inevitable spring. Action was relief. Pound,
pound, pound—legs in the air and a backward leap.
They had all popped into the holes, disappeared completely. The crosslegged nurses merely nodded ap-
proval. And the curtain fell.

The Chief of the King Islanders came out from a
door to the left of the stage. The wolf's head lay limp
in his hand. Sweat ran down his face. He stood a head
above the rest of the group and had that air of being
looked at which is quite free from any self-conscious-
ness, as though stares could reflect themselves on the
face of the person beheld even when he is unconscious
of them. The Chief did not notice the eyes turned toward him, for he was watching the sports now beginning in the hall.

Chairs pushed back, the Eskimo boys were kicking,
with both feet together, at a large ball suspended from

the rafters. Their toes often higher than their heads, they doubled up in a marvelously precise fashion like a jackknife. Now the girls' competition. The ball was lowered from the ceiling to meet their height. A thin strip of a girl was running down the aisle, her black braids tossing arrogantly. Stop, leap, and kick—the ball shot into the air and spun dizzily. That was an easy one. "The Chief's daughter," someone whispered to me. The ball was raised; the contestants fell out; one fat girl tried and sat down on the floor; everyone laughed.

There were only two left now. A run, a jump, and a leap—the ball floated serenely out of reach. Three times and out. Only the Chief's daughter left. A run, a jump, and a leap—the ball gleamed untouched. She missed it. She ran back shaking her braids. The ball was still. Several people coughed, rustled their programs. I saw her sullen little face as she turned. A run, a jump, and a leap. We could not see her touch it but the ball quivered slightly and began to spin. She had grazed it. "Hi! Hi!" shouted the Eskimos, and the crowd clapped. Her expression did not change as she wriggled back into her seat. But the Chief of the King Islanders was smiling, an easy, arrogant smile.

The next morning we walked down the plank streets of Nome to the King Islanders' camp. The town was quiet after the excitement of the night before. Life in camp was going on as usual. In the shade of their long curved "umiaks" sat whole families, mothers nursing their babies, old men filing at ivory tusks, while near by were young men curing fish, hanging long lines of them up to dry in the sun. We stopped and talked to one of the ivory filers. He had a half-finished match box in his hand. A pile of white dust lay at his feet. He was, we were to discover, the Chief's brother.

"That was a wonderful dance of yours last night." A broad smile accentuated his high cheekbones. Then gravely he looked up at us.

"My," he said simply.

" 'My,' " we echoed. "What do you mean?"

"*My*," he repeated with emphasis, putting down his file, "*my* brother, *my* son, *my* nephews—" He took a long breath. "*My*."

That was it, I thought, as we walked back. That was what the Chief of the King Islanders felt, shaking the water from his face after the somersault. That was what he thought tossing his wolf's head. That was what he meant by that smile when his daughter made the ball quiver—simply, "*My*."

ELEVEN

Kamchatka

✦

My preconceived idea of Russia was very strange. Admitting the absurdity of having "an idea" of a country as enormous and varied as Russia, it was still very strange. My impressions were drawn from the following sources: Old Régime stories of the Revolution; imposing New Régime programs; enthusiastic friends who had visited Leningrad on a tour; enthusiastic friends who had never visited Leningrad—or any other place in Russia; headlines from the newspapers; bits of gossip: "I have a friend who knows quite well one of the old ladies in waiting . . . and they say really . . . it is quite shocking . . ."; reformers who, unexpected, popped up beside me at dinner and disconcerted me by shouting vindictively from their dress suits, "And *they* were sitting eating hothouse asparagus—just like *you!*"; heated discussions about the breakdown of the home, of the sanctity of motherhood, and of marriage, which always started from the innocent question, "Are you going to send your child to

nursery school?"; posters and pictures showing strong
men swinging sledge hammers, industrious women
riveting airplane wings, and earnest children hammer-
ing blocks; the inevitable, "What would you do if this
were Soviet Russia?"; and always that man in the end
of the room, with his back to the fire, rubbing his hands
and saying mildly and benevolently at the end of all
discussions, "Well, I am sure they could teach us quite
a few things."

It was a country, as far as I could see, of workers,
stern uncompromising workers, uniformly bent on one
cause. They lived according to rigid rules, rules of
science, order, and efficiency, from which they never
deviated. Any erring from the straight path was severely punished. They cared about nothing in life
except this cause. Human relationships were trivial beside it. Happiness, pleasure, and beauty, grace, laughter, and courtesy, were all subservient to it, so I imagined. An admirable picture, but too much like my Puritan forefathers to please me. However, the Puritan
cause was freedom to worship God; and the cause of
the Soviet was—not. I did not know what it was, exactly.

And of course the Soviets were young and modern,
modern men, modern women, modern children. No, I
did not fit in there. Was I a modern woman? I flew
a modern airplane and used a modern radio but not as
a modern woman's career, only as wife of a modern
man. They would find me out, too, I was sure of that,
those Pilgrim Fathers. They were stern examiners.
Pinning me down, they would question me, "Can you
explain the theory of regeneration in the vacuum
tube?" "No." "What do you know about the inside of
this radio?" "Nothing." "What do you do to justify your
existence?" "I don't know." "Occupation?" "Married."
"Well then, we have decided to—" But what could
they do to me? After all, my husband was scientific
and orderly and efficient enough for two. In fact, if he
were not efficient and orderly, I might be more so. So,

really, it was all evened up in the end. But that argument might not convince them. It would just sound frivolous. And frivolity seemed out of my picture of the U.S.S.R. So my mind wandered as we approached the shores of Kamchatka.

This was our first port in Russia. We were flying over the little island of Karaginski before landing. It looked green in comparison to Nome, our last stop. Low bushes and trees came down to a stony beach. Jagged mountains formed a background in the distance. It could hardly be called a settlement, but there were several well-built log houses with peaked roofs and pointed chimneys. A small group stood on the beach watching us. They looked friendly, some of the men dressed in the conventional blue Russian smocks, knee breeches, and high boots, their bearded faces peering out under high caps. A few natives, and two women dressed in baggy blouses and short skirts, completed the group. Behind them ran a shaggy dog. No, as we drew nearer we saw it was a little brown bear.

Here, I thought, is where I find some use for my list of Russian words, compiled by a friend in New York. "We are Americans," "Me Amerikäntzi"—that is not bad but it hardly seems necessary. They know who we are, because they have gasoline here for us. Going on to the next sentence, "Does anyone here speak English?"—"Govorit le kto leebo zdies po Angliiski?" That looks more difficult. I wonder how you pronounce *zd*.

At this moment one of the women who had climbed into a boat greeted me in French. I pulled myself together and shouted back (It is so much easier to whisper French—poor French especially), "Je comprends le français mais je parle très peu."

"Oh," she said, smiling at me gayly, "I spik English." (Eskimos "hunt duck" in Shishmaref Inlet and Russians "spik English" in Karaginski! There are no surprises left.) Our interpreter, we discovered, was a zoölogist who was making a study of animals on the island. The rest of the inhabitants were trappers, fur trapping and fur farming apparently being the only occupation of the settlement.

Furs were everywhere in the house to which we were led. Red foxes hung in the outside hall. A big bearskin covered the heavy beamed door to the kitchen. Even in the little sitting room where we were finally taken, a bunch of ermine tails were strung up on a hook. Other decorations on the wall were pictures of a favorite cat and a piece of embroidery showing gnomes in a pine forest. That room was dining room, living room, and also, for us, bedroom. A long table and a big dresser for plates and food took up most of the space. It was here, after much bowing and questioning, we finally sat down and smiled at each other. The zoölogist introduced us to her husband and the other couple, a trapper and his wife. Conversation was difficult. We talked in bad French and bad English. She would say, "The mother bear was kiled" (to rhyme with wild), and, "He (the baby bear) was quite, quite willed" (to rhyme with killed). I do not like to think what I said. The trapper's wife went out to get fresh milk and wild strawberries and to cook some meat. Dunka, the bear, smelling food, pushed his way into the kitchen and stood up on his hind legs next to the table.

"Dunka! Dunka!" the shouts went up, as though a bad child had put his fingers into the jam. But more unmanageable than a child, with his long claws, Dunka had to be coaxed out with a piece of raw meat. Clumsily shaking from side to side, he followed the outstretched hand that held the morsel until, once outside, and the door banged in his face, he began to grunt angrily.

We sat inside enjoying our meal and tried to thank our hosts. Thinking that sweets might be as much appreciated in Kamchatka as in the North, we had brought a box of candy from Nome. They, however, placed good Soviet chocolate in front of us and the only treat we had to offer was a sandwich of fresh lettuce grown in a Nome backyard. The trapper's wife had tasted none for two years.

Suddenly the two men who had been talking to each other began to laugh. The zoölogist nodded, with sparkling eyes, and asked us, "What—day—you—leave Nome?"

"Why, we left this morning—this is Friday, isn't it?"

"Da! Da! Da!" They tipped back their chairs and shouted with laughter. "But here—Sa-tur-day!" We had passed the one hundred and eightieth meridian and lost a full day.

The next morning the zoölogist told me that she had a little boy who was in Moscow. I said I had a little boy too. "How old—is he?" "Where—is he?" The two women discussed it together in Russian, and then very shyly asked, "You have—pho-to-graph?" I took out my photographs. "Oh! Oh!" They were gay and sweet, spreading them all on the table in the room. The trapper's wife made big circles with her hands to show how big his eyes were and pointed to the photograph she liked the best. Then, picking out others, she made me understand by pointing again, "This looks most like his mother," and, "This is like his father."

When I left, my boy seemed nearer to me because they had seen his picture and had talked of him. Perhaps the zoölogist also felt closer to her boy, for she gave me a letter for him, to post in Tokyo. I had it in my pocket as we took off the next morning for Petropavlovsk in our orange and black plane—as we circled above that group of figures far below us on the beach, waving their tiny arms in a final gesture of farewell.

(I don't feel out of place here, I thought, but Petropavlovsk will be the real test.)

Petropavlovsk looked orderly and efficient enough from the air. The inner harbor was a small round gem

set in steep volcanic hills; the gray-roofed town, which
looked quite large to us after the small Northern settlements, grew in regular fashion up the side of a hill. It
was busy too, we could see that from above. Big fishing boats were turning in the toy harbor, unbelievably
deep for its size. And we could see the fresh clean wood
of new construction going up next to the shore. It
was here just below the town that we left our plane, in
the most beautiful anchorage it had yet seen.

My first sight as we boarded the wharf was of workmen. They were not swinging sledge hammers; they
had crowded on the pier to see us land and were intensely interested. They knew, of course, who my husband was. "But she, who is she!" (In Russian, of
course.) This is no place for me, I thought. How do
you justify your existence? But the officials who came
down to meet us had no questions to ask. They greeted
us gayly and cordially and pushed a way through the
crowd to a waiting car. The man at my side was con-
siderately trying to help me over mud puddles, a sur-
prising but rather unnecessary courtesy, as I was wearing trousers and very tough old shoes.

We bumped up the side of the hill, missing pigs and
children by inches as we turned through the town. The
houses bordering the road were all old and rather ram-
shackle, but still charming under their carved and gayly
painted eaves. The wooden sidewalks were crowded
with people who were not very well dressed, the
women in baggy shirtwaists and short skirts, but all of
whom looked healthy and happy and far too busy to
pay attention to us. The little town hummed with life.
Only the white church looked deserted. With windows
boarded up, it stood alone in a grass-grown yard. One
workman had found his way into this quiet spot and
had stretched out for a nap.

As we went up the hill, the houses were better. The
"best house in town" was right on the crest. "In the
old days," it was explained to us naïvely, "there was a
high priest. He lived up there"—with a nod up the

hill—"and the governor did not dare do anything without running up the street to ask his blessing. Now there
is no priest and the Zav [representative of the Com-
munist Party] lives there. When the president of the
local governing committee does not know what to do,
he can quickly find out by running up the hill"—pointing to the same house—"to ask the Zav for advice."

The government house to which we were taken was
a few doors below the Zav's house. An old wooden
building several stories high, it looked down over gray
roofs to the crescent harbor and our orange-winged
plane. We walked through a hall papered with large
posters of Lenin, Laborers, Capitalists, and Tractors,
upstairs into a corner room. Here three cots had been
placed, one separated from the other two by a flimsy
Chinese screen. "For you and your husband and the
mechanic!" (not realizing we had no mechanic).
There were two razors laid out on a table for the two
men and a bottle of perfume for me. I thought the
bottle of perfume looked slightly improper standing
between the two razors. Here we ate (all our meals
were brought to us) and slept while we were in
Petropavlovsk. And here we had our only adventure
in Russia.

It was the last night. We woke to loud shouts about
four in the morning—sharp staccato shouts falling
abruptly one on another. Then a crash of breaking
glass. My husband tumbled out of bed and ran to the
window. "That's a real yell. Either something's happened to the plane, or—there's a fire!" We could see
the orange wings riding safely in the harbor below us.
More shouts, and the smell of smoke. Fire!

"Quick, get dressed!" said my husband. "Help me
to put these things together in the blanket—here—
near the window—so we can throw them out if we
have to."

He folded up the silk screen; put it in a corner;
pushed the beds out of the way. Windows open.
Curtains rolled up. All our things in blankets near the

window. "I'll come back," he shouted, as he opened the door to the hall. Clouds of smoke pushed in as he went out. Back in a few seconds for a wet towel for his nose and mouth, "Smoke's—bad—but you can still go down the stairs—or out the window—I'll come back."

I looked out at a fifteen-foot drop. Perhaps I could get a foothold on the sill below. On the road opposite I could see men running downhill, carrying buckets of water. It seemed to me that I stood here half an hour, watching those men hurrying up and down hill, listening to disordered sounds below, footsteps running back and forth, scufflings and kickings and muffled shouts. Then out of the mêlée of undefined footsteps, certain stronger more purposeful ones came to my door —hesitated—stopped—a loud knock.

"Come in!"

A frightened-looking man flung open the door and hesitated a moment, "O-pen win-dows!"

"Yes—I have—"

Shutting the door again, he ran away.

Another wait. The voices subsided below in the street. My husband came back, laughing, "It's out." We pulled down the curtains and went back to bed. "A fire in the files downstairs," he explained; "didn't get far—but this house would go like kindling if it got started."

In a few minutes we were waked by a "Ting-a-ling" in the street below and the rattle of wheels. We looked out. A one-horse cart pulling a small tank and a wound-up hose drew up in front of the building. Two men with brass bees'-nest helmets on their heads leaped down dramatically. They shouted orders and began to unwind and couple up the hose. The fire engine!

"I don't believe, Charles, they're any more efficient than I am!"

During our visit, we did all the things that one is supposed to do in Russia before one writes about it.

We went out to an experimental farm; we saw tractors heaving up a hill. We went to look at stores and schools and some of the new construction; and we asked questions. I asked so many questions that in the end our friend, the curator, said to me, with a touch of humor, "When you write your book, please send it to me."

But I am not going to write it. As I look over the notes I took down carefully, the items, which seemed so important to me then, wither on the page. They are completely lifeless. It is not that they are unimportant. It is important that the experimental farm, literally hewn out of the mountain side, was doing well; that the chickens and cows and pigs were well bred; that the new grains were growing. It is important that a large part of the town budget went to the schools. There were three in that little town, where the children, aside from their lessons, were fed two meals a day and washed and clothed. The whole machinery of the "common" stores and the (government-owned) "commercial" stores was tremendously interesting. But if I were to write all those facts down as my impressions of Kamchatka, I would still have missed the point completely. I would have left out the most significant and real impression that remains with me. It is a difficult thing to analyze, but when I think of Russia now, I do not think of community farms and nursery schools. I think of the two women in Karaginski smiling over my baby's picture, of the men tipping back their chairs and laughing at our crossing the date line. I think of my quiet-humored little friend the curator saying to me, "When you write your book, please send it to me."

I think of people and not of ideas and plans and organizations. Perhaps, after all, I am not really a modern woman. Certainly I have no modern answer to give when I am asked—as I always am, for there has been more curiosity about those two small points we touched on the Russian Continent than about any other portion of the trip—"I hear you've been to Russia—what did you think of it?"

I can only protest childishly, "It isn't *It;* it's *Them,* and I like them."

TWELVE

Fog—and the Chishima

❖

"Wel-come - - - to - - - Japan - - - wel-come - - - Colonel - - - Lindbergh - - -" I was taking down my first message from JOC, the Japanese radio station at Nemuro which had followed us painstakingly down the Siberian coast and which was to guide us to Tokyo. Technically, we were in Japan then, following the Chishima, that chain of islands which links the Kamchatka Peninsula to Hokkaido. This must be Buroton Bay (I consulted a chart), this little harbor here, cupped in a green volcano. It looked like a miniature "Japanese garden"—the toy house with grass-covered roof set by the side of the bay, a minute flat-bottomed boat gingerly floating in the water. Typical, I thought. And those volcanic peaks—they were typical too—rising sharply from the sea, with bits of fog clinging to their sides. Every Japanese print, I remembered, had a fog-draped volcano in the background.

The notes buzzed ahead in my ears, "Wel-come - - - Colonel - - - Lindbergh - - - to Japan!" How typical, also, to have our first message from Japan one of pure grace, not utilitarian in any sense, merely a bow of welcome before we got down to the business of position and weather. They were as interested as we in the business of position and weather, but the bow came first—the eternal gentleman!

The weather was important. For some time we had

noticed a long low fog bank to the east. Far out to sea,
like a second horizon, this even white line stretched
ahead, paralleling our course. It did not seem at first
to be approaching but rather, keeping step with us
cautiously, to be warning us off, marking a boundary
we must not overstep. Gradually, however, it pushed
us back more and more to a course directly over the
islands instead of the one originally prescribed, fifteen
miles east of these "fortified areas."

Looking ahead now I could see that the line of fog
and the line of the islands were converging. Like a long
wave on a shoal, the clouds of mist seemed to break
over the barrier of these volcanic peaks. Was it an accidental infringement, I wondered, like that unusually
high wave on a rocky beach, which oversteps the wa-
terline and wets the stones under your feet? Or was it
actually a turn in the tide? Would our stepping-stones
be entirely covered? I looked down on the fairylike
peaks, pushing their heads up through the mist, floating on mist now, like a child's dessert. Every now and
then we could see through a hole in the clouds a rocky
beach or a strip of hare-bell-blue water gleam and van-
ish. A melting, shimmering, unreal world, too beautiful to be menacing.

"Pse (Please) - - - send - - - wea (weather) - - -
speed - - - posn (position)" ticked my next message
from JOC. I would have to be practical. But I did not
know where we were. "Flying - - - through - - - fog,"
I tapped back. "Will - - - send - - - posn - - - in - - - minute." There was nothing accidental or slight about
those clouds. They stretched on and on, now, an even
sea ahead of us. They were still rather low; we could
go above them—if there were good weather to go to.
But the sky beyond was gray. What did that mean,
more fog—or storm?

"Is - - - it - - - clear - - - at - - - Nemuro? - - - what
- - - ceiling - - - and - - - visibility - - - pse?" We reached
out for word of good weather ahead, like a helping
hand to pull us across that chasm of bad weather be-

low. How far down did the peaks descend? Could they be judged like icebergs? Was there twice as much—three times as much—below the surface? The fog would never give us an answer, I knew that. Too often before I had watched it like frozen foam on the sides of mountains. Smiling, still and bright, it never gave one an inkling of what was hidden below. I felt fear creeping imperceptibly over me, as cold does at night when, half asleep, one refuses to recognize it. "No—I am not cold," one says. "I don't need to reach down and pull up that other blanket—*something* is wrong, but I'm not *cold*." So I fought off recognition of fear and only thought, "It was a lovely day when we started. . . ." "The sun is shining up above the clouds. . . ." "Nemuro says it is clear there. . . ." "It's still open behind us—isn't it?" But before I had time to look, my husband pushed back a message to me, "Fog on sea extends upward several thousand feet —storm clouds ahead—we are turning back and will land at first opportunity—now over southwest end Shimushiru To."

I started relaying to Nemuro, "Fog - - - on - - - sea" (smiling, still and bright) - - - "storm - - - clouds - - - ahead" (that dark curtain shut right down to the south) - - - "we - - - are - - - turning - - - back" (the great wing wheeled below me in the clouds) - - - "will - - - land - - -" (It was just as dark behind us! We *never* came through that. It had shut in on us!) - - - "at - - - first - - - opportunity" (one green peak pushed its head above the fog).

"Are - - - you - - - turning - - - back - - - to - - - land?" came the answer quickly. "Most - - - advisable - - - Buroton - - - Bay." Buroton Bay—that miniature Japanese-garden harbor that we had passed when it was clear. Now it would be closed in by fog. We could never find it again. How safe it had looked half an hour ago, the hut set down neatly by the water's edge, the boat calmly poised in the water. We were in another world now, separated from that idyllic one by an

impenetrable layer of fog. It was still there, though.
That man in the radio station at Nemuro had found it
on the map. It was comforting to feel that he could
find it even if we could not. He knew where we were,
too, and where we should go. Like an omniscient god,
"There," he said, his finger on the map, "Buroton
Bay—land there." If only he could place us there as
in a giant chess game.

My husband pushed back the cockpit cover, put
on his helmet and goggles, heightened the seat for
better visibility, and leaned forward to look out. Here
we are again, I thought, recognizing by this familiar
buckling-on-of-armor that the fight had begun.

Here we are again. We seem to be always here, I
thought, fear opening for me a long corridor of similar
times and making them all one long fight with
fog. There was the time over the Alleghenies in the
Falcon: slicing over the tops of those pine trees, now
on one wing, now on another. Then we found the river
down below the mist cutting a gully through the mountains. We followed it and came out to safety. But then
with a *Falcon* it wasn't so dangerous—not so fast. The
Sirius now— (He was headed for that peak in the
clouds. How did he know there was not a lower peak
—a shoal, just covered by this high tide of fog—that
might trip us up as we skimmed across the surface?)
Then, there had been that time over the pass of the
San Bernardino Mountains. "Ceiling, very low," read
the weather report. "What does 'very low' mean?" my
husband had asked. "Two or three hundred feet?"

"It means nothing at all," laughed the weather man.
"You'd better stay here."

"Oh, we'll go see what it looks like—may come
back—may find a hole." And up we had climbed until
we were face to face with those giants, snow-streaked,
and the bright fog sitting on their shoulders. But that
time, too, finally we struck a stream and followed it—a
beautiful stream with fields to land in and green or-
chards and houses. It carried us along and spilled us

out into the broad valley of San Bernardino. I had it like a ribbon in my hand all through the fog. I held on to it and it led us out.

Here there was nothing to hold on to—nothing, unless it were the sky. The sun still shone. My husband motioned me to reel in the antenna. Emergency landing, that meant. I buckled my belt tighter. We were circling the giant's head now, getting impudently nearer and nearer. Down, down, we were gliding down now, the engine throttled, wisps of fog temporarily blinding us as we descended. I was losing the sky. I did not want to let go until I could grasp something below. Down the sides of the mountain one could see a strip of water gleaming, hare-bell-blue. We were diving toward it. Down, down—the sky was gone. The sea! Hold on to the sea—that little patch of blue. Oh, the sea was gone too. We were blind—and still going down—oh, God!—we'll hit the mountain! A wave of fear like terrific pain swept over me, shriveling to blackened ashes the meaningless words "courage"—"pride" —"control." Then a lurch, the engine roared on again, and a sickening roller-coaster up. Up, up, up. I felt myself gasping to get up, like a drowning man. There —the sky was blue above—the sky and the sun! Courage flowed back in my veins, a warm, pounding stream. Thank God, there is the sky. Hold on to it with both hands. Let it pull you up. Oh, let us stay here, I thought, up in this clear bright world of reality, where we can see the sky and feel the sun. Let's never go down.

He is trying it again, like a knife going down the side of a pie tin, between fog and mountain. Will he say afterward, "It was nothing at all"? (if there is an "afterward"). That time in the Alleghenies he turned around, when we struck the river, and smiled at me. It was so reassuring. If only he would do it now. But his face was set. I could see it out of the side of the cockpit— his lips tight-closed. The force of the wind blowing against them made them look thin and fearful like a man gritting his teeth in his last fight. Were we there, then, at the last fight? I had never seen him look like that. The wind flattened his face, made the flesh flabby, the brows prominent—like a skeleton.

Down again—and the terror. Up again—and the return of courage and shame. Think of the radio operators sticking to their posts through fire and flood. If only I could send messages, it would help. Think of the air-mail pilots, doing this every night. Think of the war pilots to whom weather was the smallest of their worries. At least weather was impersonal; it had no ax to grind. Think of that old lady in the early days of flying who took her first transcontinental trip fearlessly —how calmly she said, "Tonight I will be in Clovis— or Heaven." Why not accept it philosophically, like that, "Buroton Bay or Heaven," and not struggle through all the intervening stages of fear? But Buroton Bay did not sound like safety to me. It sounded like one of those quiet, unmarked places which, because of an accident, suddenly become steeped with tragedy: "Crashed—south side Buroton Bay." "Buroton Bay" —the name rings crimson like the name of an old battlefield.

Why try Buroton Bay anyway? Why not go somewhere else—anywhere else? Oh, I realized suddenly, that was what he was doing. The giant was floating behind us in the mist now, getting dimmer and dimmer as new veils of mist separated us. Ahead, I could see nothing—but above, the blue sky and the sun. "The sun is shining free of charge," jingled in my mind flippantly. I felt quite gay. After all, we weren't killed. We're still here in this blue sky—and "the sun is shining free of charge." Oh, Lord—here was another mountain peak! Was he going to try it again? Hadn't he learned *anything*? Did he think I really enjoyed this game of tobagganing down volcanoes? I thought in a kind of bravado anger. Really it was too much—I would never fly again. The sun began to melt away as we spiraled down. It became a thin watery disk in

the mist. "Never fly again," echoed in my ears mali-
ciously. No—never fly again—I had said it myself and
shivered to think how true it might be. Down, down,
into the darkness. We had never been down this far
before. That long green slope at the foot of the volcano—could we make a forced landing there? Bushes
and rocks—but still the pontoons would take up the
shock. It would be wonderful to be down—even there.
No—we were going too fast, skimming over the bushes
and straight down the slope. For there, over a sharp
cliff of fifty feet, under a layer of mist, lay the water.
There it was, shifting, changing, hiding tantalizingly
below us. That was what we wanted. If we could only
lay our hands on it before it disappeared—like the
stone one dives for in the bottom of a pool. Could we
reach it or would we have to fight our way up again?
We dropped off the cliff. We were over the water.
Spank, spank, spank—the ship is breaking under us! I
am falling through. No—the seat has bounced down,
that's all. It must be rough water. We're slowing up
now. We're all right—we're down!

My husband turned around for the first time and
looked at me. "What's the matter?"

"Nothing," I stammered. "I'm so happy to be
down."

He laughed. "We weren't in much danger. We could
have gone back; but I was trying to get into Buroton
Bay. I don't like to anchor in open water—going to try
to find a more sheltered spot."

I pushed the cockpit cover all the way open and
looked out. The idling motor whined, a peculiarly des-
olate and lonely sound, like the wind around a house
at night. I could hear the waves crashing against the
shore. There was nothing to see except fog. How did
we ever get down!

We began to taxi slowly, creeping in toward the
island. I could make out the shore line now—a rocky
coast, the dark mass of a hill behind rising up—how
far into the mist? For we were under that sea of fog

now, irrevocably separated from the sky above. And this submarine world was as strange and confusing as the world above. Where were we? Where were we going? Was that really the shore line? The fog blowing in would blot it out altogther at times, and we had to keep near to see it. As we drew closer, the crashing waves on the rocks warned us off. What was this conspiracy against us? The big sea-swell bobbed our ship up and down. And what was this dark stuff we were plowing through? Seaweed—pushing up over the floats, twining around the rudders, forcing them up until they banged back, protesting. Here and there across the water I could see great coils of seaweed rising from the surface like some strange sea monster. This was an enchanted place—a Sargasso Sea. What unearthly creatures might not be on that island. I strained my eyes to see. Were those rounded huts? We drew nearer. No, only bowlders. The sea crashed against the shore; the engine whined on and on. What time was it? We had been an hour out of communication. I began to think of home. Would there be crash rumors out? What was my last message? "Will land at first opportunity." What would the Japanese say to our landing? Bang, bang! The rudders went up over the seaweed. How slowly we were going. There was no sign of life—only the roar of that wash on the shore and the whine of the motor.

Finally we reached the lee side of the island, cut the engine, and threw down our anchor. Now for JOC. We strung the antenna out along the wing and called, "JOC - - - JOC - - -" Oh, there he was, "KHCAL - - - QRK (I can hear you well; your signals are good) - - - GA (go ahead) - - -"

"Forced - - - down - - - by - - - fog," I started. "Unable - - - to - - - land - - - at - - - Buroton - - - Bay - - - due - - - to - - - fog—anchored - - - in - - - open - - - ocean - - - 200 - - - meters - - - off - - - south - - - east - - - shore - - - Ketoi - - - Island—visibility - - - on - - - water - - - 300 - - - meters—is - - - stormy - - - weather

- - - expected - - - tonight?" As I stopped sending, I could hear him rattling off to another station news of our safe arrival.

"OK - - - OK," came back the answer. "Here - - - is - - - not - - - stormy - - - weather - - - expected." Typical, I thought, smiling at the inverted phrase—not stopping to consider that had they sent in Japanese, I would have understood nothing. "Here - - - is - - - calm—what - - - time - - - you - - - landed - - - pse?" (How good to get that word. I felt relieved.)

"Landed - - - 07.45 - - - GMT (Greenwich mean time)," I answered. "Will - - - proceed - - - to - - - Nemuro - - - in - - - morning - - - if - - - clear - - - otherwise - - - Buroton - - - Bay—will - - - call - - - u (you) - - - in - - - morning - - - thank - - - u."

"We - - - arranged - - - Shinshiru—Maru (how could they have arranged anything so quickly, I marveled, as I took down the next message) - - - to - - - come - - - Buroton - - - Bay - - - in - - - one - - - or - - - two - - - hours."

I handed this forward to my husband. How nice, I thought. I didn't know what Shinshiru Maru was, but it was something "to assist us" and that sounded encouraging. However, he dictated the answer.

"Thank - - - you - - - greatly - - - appreciate - - - consideration (just like one of his typewritten notes; I would recognize that anywhere)—however - - - unless - - - emergency - - - arises - - - will - - - not - - - require - - - assistance. (How very male, I thought, regretfully, now I will never know who Shinshiru Maru is.) "Will - - - call - - - u - - - in - - - ten - - - hours - - - if - - - OK - - - with - - - u."

"OK," came back the answer. Well, that was all settled then. We were down; safe; anchored. We had communicated with JOC. We could now settle down for the night. The wind whined around us and fog curled over the wings. Water sucked gently under the pontoons. Warm and dry under the curved dome of our fuselage, we would be quickly rocked to sleep.

What was that? Something else? He was still sending?
I jotted down the letters, "We - - - welcome - - - eagerly - - - you - - - here - - - tomorrow - - - good - - -
evening - - - remember - - - me - - - to - - - Colonel
- - - Lindbergh." The eternal gentleman!

THIRTEEN

The Singing Sailors

❀

I was just finishing my radio schedule the next morning when—there they were! Around the corner came
the sailors, singing as they rowed, their round pudding
sailor caps bobbing up and down. (Just like the caps
little boys used to wear in the parks in Germany, only
the sailors had no ribbons down their backs.) They
were headed directly for us and seemed to come from
nowhere, appearing on the scene appropriately like a
Gilbert and Sullivan chorus: "Enter, right, eight singing
sailors." But where from? We looked over the wing
and saw, sitting calmly two hundred meters away from
us, a two-masted ship, already well settled with anchor down, clothes hung out to dry, and cooking smoke
trailing out of the galley. Had this risen out of the mist
or had it been there all night? It had come in so quietly.
As the wind swung the stern around, I read under the
Japanese characters, *Shinshiru Maru*. ("Will send
Shinshiru Maru Buroton Bay to assist you"—that was
the message last night from JOC.) Of course, this was
the *Shinshiru Maru* we said we did not need. Wisely
enough, they had sent it anyway. I started to radio that
it had arrived.

At this moment the eight singing sailors were easing
up to the pontoons. A little officer (the radio operator,

we learned later) rose to get out, bowed to us, put his foot on the pontoon, and, looking for something to hold on to, reached for the antenna wire. We shouted, but the little radio operator, who had received a four-hundred-volt shock, showed neither pain nor fright. He merely backed away and smiled apologetically. "What," he said with restraint, "ah—ah—ees—*that?*" We explained what it was, and quickly turned off the power, taking no chance on his touching it again as he climbed up the side of the plane. After he had inspected the cockpit with delight, "Ah—ah—ah—" He cleared his throat and began formally, "You—ah—ah—have—ah —*cohee?*"

My husband, not sure what he meant, reached down and hopefully handed him one of our soft sea-soaked cookies. Our friend bowed, smiled, and politely swallowed the cookie.

Then he started again, "You—ah—ah—have *cohee?*"

Charles: "Have *what?*"

Radio operator: "*Cohee*—on—sheep," pointing to the *Shinshiru Maru* and smiling.

Charles: "Coffee—oh, yes—coffee!" We were all smiles.

(My husband, reading over my shoulder, denies this story. "I offered the cookie to him to be polite," he says, "and I thought it might suggest breakfast!")

In the warm little cabin of the *Shinshiru Maru* we were brought the delicious luxury of hot water and soap in a brass basin, a comb, cold cream, and even, out of the handsome Captain's own drawer, hair pomade. Then at last, toast and "cohee." After breakfast we thanked them enthusiastically and, shaking hands all around, we started back to our plane, hoping to take off in the clearing mist. The singing sailors helped us lash a spar to a bent pontoon strut, and then rowed away.

We were ready to start. The climbing whine of the inertia-starter, the grind of the clutch, the engine catching for a moment, and then—splutter, putt, putt—

dying away. That was the only response we could get
over and over again. It was cold and wet. A strong wind
blew down over the slope of the island, covering every
thing with mist and salt spray. The sailors on the
Shinshiru Maru watched us from the rail of the boat.

Suddenly we noticed that the distance between us
and the boat was increasing. Were we drifting? The
anchor rope was slack. My husband jumped down from
the cockpit and began pulling at it. It came easily, too
easily. The frayed end jumped out of the water; the
anchor was gone. A sharp edge of rock, chafing all
night on our rope, had cut it free. We were adrift, not
more than a hundred feet from the breakers off a rocky
coast, and no hope of starting the engine. We raised
our arms and shouted for help. The sailors had already
started in their boat, straining at the oars but still
breathlessly keeping time with their chant. Quickly
and efficiently they caught us as we drifted toward
the rocks, made us fast to their own anchor, and rowed
away smiling. "Will send *Shinshiru Maru* to assist you"
—the message had come true.

As a matter of fact, we became even more dependent
on them. Our battery was almost run down by constant
efforts to start the engine. We did not want to exhaust
it completely by sending radio messages unless an emergency arose. We must wait for the engine to recharge
it. But we could not start our engine. My husband
thought the trouble lay in some fouled spark plugs,
caused by taxiing the night before. He would have to
clean them before we could start. The rain and salt
water had also thoroughly soaked every part of the
engine, which did not make matters easier.

All this we tried to explain to the radio operator on
his next trip to the plane. It took a long time, almost
all morning. He had a way of smiling and saying, "Ah—
ah," politely and reassuringly after each sentence, as
though understanding everything. But he invariably
turned, as he was about to leave, with a question which
started us back at the very beginning of our expla-

nations, "Radio—ah—ah—broke—please?" It is not strange that word went back home that our engine, our radio, and our anchor were broken. It might as well have been so. It was too rough and wet to work on the engine; we had to send messages through their radio; and we were using their anchor.

And by afternoon we were also smelling their food. A delicious odor of fried fish had been drifting back to us for hours from their galley. We had not eaten a full meal for twenty-four hours, though we had carried sandwiches, cookies, and chocolate from Petropavlovsk, and we were beginning to be hungry. Surely they would ask us for lunch on the ship! They were so hospitable. Any moment the singing sailors might appear. We waited and waited. My husband got out the engine instruction book and started reading to pass the time away. I watched the ship. No sign of life on the *Shinshiru Maru*. Still that delicious smell. "What do you think it is, Charles? Fried fish and buttered rice?" We waited and waited. "I think they're coming now—no—they're just mopping up the deck."

Of course we did have food of our own, not only emergency army rations, but cans of good baked beans and tomatoes. But to cook anything, we would have to unpack our rubber boat, inflate it, get out the oars, row to shore, set up our Primus stove, and by that time—surely they would ask us to lunch! Still no sign of the singing sailors. I brought out my book of radio calls and some notes on the weather in Kamchatka and the Chishima. "Average days of fog in August—twenty-eight"! Heavens, it was already the twentieth of August. We might have missed the three good days; we would be there forever. And still no lunch!

At three o'clock we decided to open a can of baked beans and some biscuits. They might be short of food; probably that was why they had not asked us. After all they had done enough already; we would provide our own food. Cold baked beans spread on biscuit is very good. We had just finished the can when we heard the

knock of oars and the slow chant of the sailors! Guiltily
we licked the crumbs off our lips and jumped up.

"You—ah—eat—ah—with—us—ah—on—sheep?"
bowed the little operator.

We said nothing about the baked beans, hid our
smiles and our crumbs, and accepted. I was right about
the fish and rice, but I had not guessed that they would
offer us some especially prepared egg-powder scram-
bled eggs and canned ham, and two Western forks instead of chopsticks.

Our second night on the plane was not a comfortable
one. The Japanese had asked us to sleep in their boat,
but we refused, knowing they were crowded, and also
wishing to keep careful watch of the plane in case of
storm. Sleeping in the plane was not necessarily un-
comfortable. There was plenty of room in the big
baggage compartment, where, before we had the pontoon tanks, a two-hundred-gallon gasoline tank had
once fitted. The small door in the side of the ship,
through which the baggage was passed, made a perfect
window.

Our equipment, neatly packed on the floor in layers
according to degrees of softness, made a comfortable
bed. Everything was used, even the oars of our rubber boat, the tool-kit, the cans of emergency food, and
our canteens. For there was a big hole to fill between
the wing-spars in order to bring the level of our bunk
flush with the level of the cockpit floor boards, and
thereby lengthen it. We were careful to put the oars
and the cans at the bottom. First, the oars; then, the
tool-kit and spare parts of the engine, the cans of food,
the bulky canvas bags of emergency equipment, the
rubber boat, the tent roll, extra coils of rope; next, our
parachute packs; then our blanket rolls of clothing; our
two flying suits for a top mattress; and, lastly, the sleeping bag. It is strange with all that stuffing that I often
felt, like *The Princess and the Pea*, acutely conscious
of the tool-kit in the small of my back. Still one usually
slept, tool-kit or no tool-kit.

But not this night.

A tornado swept the sea to the west. The wind broke over the mountain top and tore past us, kicking up a choppy sea even on the lee shore. The plane tossed and tossed, and we with it, rolling from one side of the fuselage to the other. The little window banged open and shut with each lurch and in the whistle of the cowlings I seemed to hear the strange note of the radio. Faint whistlings, too fast for me to copy, ran through my brain, tantalizingly. Suddenly in the nightmare of noise we heard what sounded like a human wail or chant. My husband crawled back to the cockpit, opened the hatch, and peered out into the darkness. The rain beat on his face but he was able to see a small light bobbing up and down on the water—the singing sailors! What could bring them out on a night like this? Were we dragging anchor? Perhaps they had some warning message. The tornado—had it shifted its course? Was it driving toward us? He watched the light slowly draw nearer and the boat appear, black against the black water. The sailors were pulling with all their strength against the waves, struggling to reach us. Clinging to the pontoon, one of them managed to reach up and hand my husband an envelope. He tore it open and read by flashlight: "The Japanese people eagerly welcome you to Japan and await your safe arrival."

"Is that all?" shouted my husband.

Apparently they could not hear him in the wind, but as they seemed to be waiting for an answer, he scribbled one and handed it down. Still incredulous he climbed back inside the plane. "Don't tell me they came through this storm just to give us a radio message!" We discovered the next morning that, worried about our safety, they had come to attach a two-inch hawser from their boat to our plane; the radiogram was thrown in "extra."

That was the last night we spent in open ocean. The next day we were towed to the long-looked-for Buroton Bay. I sat on the deck of the *Shinshiru Maru* and watched the plane ride the waves like a gull, with my husband seated on its back. It was evening when we finally reached our destination, that harbor scooped out of a round volcano which had gleamed tantalizingly below us so many hours before. "Most advisable Buroton Bay," had ticked the radio. "Crashed Buroton Bay" had echoed in my mind the day we had roared down the misty sides of that peak in an attempt to land. But now we were here. The choppy waves stilled to mirrored waters, once inside the narrow entrance. The steep volcanic sides encircled us and drew us in. The rocky beach, the thatch-roofed house, the little boat, were all there just as we had seen them in miniature from the air, only, by some miracle, we had been reduced to the same toy-village size.

But the next morning we were giants again in seven-league boots. The engine, roaring anew after a few hours' work in calm water, lifted us easily into the air. Once more the harbor dwarfed to Japanese-garden proportions. The trees became moss; the rocks, pebbles; the thatch-roofed house, a child's toy. And these tiny doll-like figures in a miniature boat, waving matchstick arms—who were they? Of course, the singing sailors.

FOURTEEN

A Fisherman's Hut

❁

"Once upon a time there was a poor fisherman who lived on the side of a lake. He had a small thatch-roofed hut which sheltered three: himself, his aged father, and a young son who helped him in his work. Every morning they poled out on the lake in their flat-bot-

tomed sampan and every evening pushed back into
the reeds with their catch; and life was never any different from day to day. One stormy evening the fisherman was out in the boat as was his custom, when he
heard a great noise in the sky. A giant bird was circling
his small hut. As he stood gazing at it, it came down on
the lake in front of his home, and a man and a woman
climbed down off its back and began to talk in strange
language."

"Where do you think we are?"

"I haven't the slightest idea," answered my husband, as he raised himself out of the cockpit, "but it
was pretty thick over Nemuro—and we are running
short of gas. This looks like a good place for the night.
I think there's a hut over there, too."

We had set out in clear weather that afternoon on
our third attempt to reach Nemuro. Finding it covered
with fog, we had turned around, come down through
a hole in the clouds, and landed here—somewhere in
the Chishima or Thousand Islands of Japan. It was
raining hard, and in the bad weather it was difficult
to tell if we were on a lake or an inlet. The body of
water was long and narrow, and sprinkled with small
grassy islands. Some willows and reeds grew along the
banks, with pine trees on the gentle ridge behind.
Whether ocean or more ridges lay beyond, we could
not see. But certainly that was a hut at the further end.
A few blasts of the engine and we were coasting toward
it. As we approached, a small sampan pushed out from
the reeds. A man was poling it. In bare feet and poorly
dressed, his ragged trousers rolled up above his knees,
he stood up and bowed a greeting to us. We smiled
and waved back at him.

"Do you speak English?"

Only another bow and smile answered us. We were
silent for a moment, wondering what medium to try
next for communication. He was quicker than we were.
Pointing to his little hut, he plainly asked us to come in

out of the rain. We smiled again and thanked him.
Motioning, in our turn, to the plane, we tried to make
him understand that there were things to be done first.
We wanted to tell the radio station at Nemuro where
we were. But where were we? My husband took a map
of the Chishima in his hand and climbed down on to
the pontoon next to the sampan. He beckoned to the
fisherman and together they looked at the map which
spoke its own language.

"Where are we?" we tried to ask, pointing to the
lake and to the map. The little fisherman obligingly put
his finger on the lower part of the Chishima group,
Kunashiri Island.

"Kunashiri?" asked my husband, pointing to the lake.
The man smiled and said something in assent.

We were all elated at our success in communicating
an idea—to have touched hands across the barrier of
incomprehension. Stringing the antenna out under the
wing, I called to JOC, "Impossible - - - to - - - land - - -
Nemuro - - - due - - - fog - - - landed - - - Kunashiri
- - - Island - - - weather - - - permitting - - - will - - -
proceed - - - Nemuro - - - in - - - morning."

The fisherman did not show any curiosity about the
radio. He sat in his boat at a respectful distance while
the dynamotor hummed in the plane. But when we
started to push toward shore, he climbed out of his
boat and waded up above his knees to help us. The
keel of the pontoons stopped at last in the mud bottom,
and the nose in the reeds. We made the anchor fast
to the bank and tied the wing-tips to willow stumps.
Our plane looked so snugly tethered, I wondered if
there were enough slack in the bridle to let it nibble at
the young willow shoots at its feet.

The little fisherman must have felt our job was finished, for he again repeated his invitation, pointing to
his boat and the hut. This time we nodded and stepped
down into the sampan. He poled us away from the
bank and, pushing through the reeds, brought us up a
small canal right to his door. Two pairs of wooden clogs

animal metaphor

on the sill reminded us gently that, according to Japanese custom, we must take off our muddy boots before entering. Leaving them behind us, we padded into the house in wool socks.

In the center of the one perfectly bare room was a smoldering charcoal fire on a hearth. Beside it sat an old man in a kimono, smoking a long white pipe. He took the pipe out of his mouth and bowed to us from his knees. A young boy came in the door behind us, also in a kimono. We all bowed to each other and sat down in dignity and silence. Our host then asked us, making a gesture of eating with chopsticks, whether we were hungry. We shook our heads. My husband, being cautious, thought they might have some infectious disease; and I, not seeing anything to eat, was trying to be as polite as the fisherman. Silence again. Now it was our turn. My husband took out his map. It had been successful before. Perhaps it would be again.

"We come from *America*," he said, making the "America" very loud and clear. Our three hosts, squatted by the fire, listened politely, but there was no flash of recognition in the expression.

Still polite silence.

"Amérique—les Etats Unis—Estados Unidos," I began hopefully, trying the only languages I knew.

The Japanese only looked a little perplexed. My husband began to draw his own map. "Siberia," he said. "Siberia—Alaska—Canada—United States—"

The Japanese turned their attention to his map. The names meant nothing.

"New York—" He set a point down.

"Ah!" cried the boy, his face lighting up with recognition, "Noo Yawk." Then they all talked together excitedly.

By that time my husband had finished his map. He set it down on the floor in our midst and pointed with his pencil, "New York—Canada—Alaska—Siberia—Kamchatka—Chishima—Kunashiri—" of which they understood only New York and Kunashiri. Satisfied with our achievement, we put our wet feet up against the fire and all smiled. The rain beat steadily on the thatched roof; the old man sucked quietly on his pipe; the young boy rose and slipped out of the room with soft deft steps. He came back with a catch of fish he had left outside the door.

Whether or not it was the sight of the fish that changed his mind, my husband began to feel at this point that no one had any infectious diseases and that he was hungry.

"Wait a minute," I said, pulling a piece of paper out of my pocket, "I can say it." I had a list of Japanese words that the innkeeper had given me in Shana, our last stop. Easy phrases, phonetic spelling. "Shoku-motsu?" ("Food?") I read out carefully. They listened politely but turned to my husband as if to say, "Please translate for us." Using his pencil again, he drew a large fish, profile view, with one round eye in the head. Turning it around for inspection, he pointed at the same time to his mouth.

"Ah," of course they understood and jumped up smiling to get a little crock of cooked fish and potatoes which sat on a shelf above our heads. It was put on the fire for warming and given to us in two rice bowls with two pairs of smooth bone chopsticks. The boy scooped some rice out of a deep canister on the side of the hearth to add to our meal. And, as a crowning luxury, the fisherman opened a little can on the shelf and took out some tea leaves. We were both given, with the greatest ceremony, a small handleless bowl of tea, which we cupped in the palms of our hands gratefully.

I took out my list of words again. "Oishi!" ("De-licious!") I said enthusiastically, which, with my smiles, and pointing to the fish, and my obvious enjoyment of the food, could hardly be misunderstood.

When we had finished, the old man bent forward from his corner and, in a gesture of great dignity, took his pipe out of his mouth and offered it to us. We tried to express, shaking our heads and smiling at the same time, our extreme appreciation but our decided regret.

We felt that it was time to go. Reading from my list again (I am an optimistic person) I said, "Tsukareta" ("We are tired"), with appropriate actions, the head drooping and the eyes closed; "toko" ("bed"), putting my head down on my hands; "hikoki" ("airplane"), pointing to the door. We did not know whether the Japanese understood the gesture or the words. It is true that they rose and ushered us out politely. But when, elated at my success, I stopped at the door and said plainly, "Arigato" ("Thank you"), they only looked perplexed and turned again to my husband for a translation. Unfortunately, "Thank you" cannot be drawn.

I continued to say it, however, that evening, rowing back to our home in the reeds, and the next morning before taking off. I said it constantly, with all variations and accent. At last, just as we were about to leave, the fisherman seemed to understand. He smiled broadly, and said, "Ah! *Arigato*," as though he had pulled an absolutely new word out of his mind, "Ah, arigato, arigato!" He bowed and smiled and we took off on that success.

I have never been quite sure, however, that this act, feigning recognition of the word, was not just a last exquisite gesture of hospitality.

FIFTEEN

The Paper and String of Life

❁

When I was a little girl I had a present brought me from Japan. The box was done up in white velvety paper and tied with a red and white paper string.

Under the neat angles of the bow was a gay paper decoration like a small red fan. When I took off the paper and string I found a wooden box, soft and smooth as a chestnut shell. Around the silken wood was a heavy silk cord firmly fastened. The lid of the box opened with a sigh, as wood brushed wood gently passing, and revealed the most exquisite doll I had ever seen. I cannot remember her now but I remember folding up the paper, the string, the fan, and the cord and tucking them all inside the box to keep forever. They seemed to me just as beautiful and precious as the doll herself.

Long afterward on my first flying visit to Japan I thought of this present. The same quality which had delighted me as a child ran like golden thread through our many impressions and linked them together—a quality which I tried to analyze. For although there were many other characteristics of the Japanese that might be as admirable, this was the one I envied most. In every Japanese there was an artist. His touch was everywhere, not only in the treasures of his museum but in his simplest kimono, in the signs his brush made writing, in the blue and red parasols that blossomed in the street on rainy days, in the most everyday dishes for his food. I began to realize that even the "paper and string" of life was transformed by his touch.

We were walking down a street in Japan. A woman in a blue cotton kimono with a baby strapped to her back stood on a corner. It was raining and a big blue and white paper umbrella was over her shoulder—a circle of white in a circle of blue behind her head, "like a halo," said my friend. Every woman had one. It is the most common kind of umbrella. We stopped in front of a small tea-house, walked down a narrow path bordered by a bamboo fence. We did not arrive at the door too abruptly and were met there by our Japanese hostess, who was on her knees bowing a low greeting. We took off our shoes on the wooden ledge outside the door and walked in stockinged feet, over the shining straw matting, up polished steps into the tea-room.

The tea-room—matted floor, walls of sliding paper doors, a porch on two sides—was empty and cool. There were cushions for us to sit on. "You must have a seat of honor"; they led me to a cushion facing the fourth wall of the room, in which there was an alcove, the Tokonoma. Here was a hanging scroll with a painting, appropriate to the coming season, of the seven autumn grasses. (Are there really lovelier grasses in Japan than anywhere else in the world, or is it because the artist in the Japanese sees them, singles them out, and shows them to us?) Tea in small blue teacups that fitted into the curve of the hand. The Japanese maid came in again bowing low at the door of the room. She had fans for us. On each fan was painted a flower or a spray of grass. We sat on our cushions and listened to the trees brushing against the porch and the cries of boys in the park below us, chasing dragon flies with long pointed bamboo sticks.

"Do you know the Japanese poem (*Hokku*) about the mother whose little boy had died?" My friend repeated it:

> How far in chase today
>   I wonder
> Has gone my Hunter
>   Of the dragon fly!

We went down to the park, walked through a little nursery between rows of potted chrysanthemum plants and dwarfed pine trees. A woman was bargaining with the gardener for a piece of vine, half as big as her finger, for her miniature Japanese garden. It was just what she wanted to climb up the stone in her dish.

I looked with wonder on the Japanese appreciation of all small things in nature. Is it because their country, beautifully and theatrically mountainous, hardly ever allows a long vista, letting them always see things at close range? Or have her strange and lovely mists some part in teaching them to see, falling often like a backdrop behind a single pine, separating it from the rest of the world? Or have the Japanese, from generations spent in one-story paper houses, learned a language, an alphabet of beauty in nature, that we, in our houses of brick and stone, have shut out? Or is it, again, only because they are always artists and see more than we do?

We were in one of their museums. The Japanese gentleman who was showing us paintings unrolled one of the scrolls, an ink sketch of one branch of a cherry tree. "Do you see," he said, "how the artist has painted the young shoots pricking off from the old branch? There is so much more life in them. You can see the new sap running in them—here is another." He unrolled a scroll and hung it on the wall in front of me. This was a water color. In the left-hand corner of the canvas, a bird ruffled and wet by the rain, a few tufts of grass and flowering weed. The rest of the canvas, bare. But although bare, it was not empty. Crowded with space, I felt paradoxically that it was the most important part of the painting, like those silences in a conversation which are so powerful that words against them flicker feebly, as stars against the wealth of blackness at night. And yet in the painting, although bird and grass were in a way dwarfed by this space, they were also set apart by it. Washed in space, they stood out, vivid and alone, a halo of stillness about them. Perhaps, I thought, this is how the Japanese see everything in nature, always with a halo of stillness, and therefore always beautiful.

This appreciative vision, which saw beauty in the smallest things and made beauty in the most trivial acts, which shone through and illuminated the paper and string of life, seemed to me to find its most vivid expression in the Tea Ceremony.

The Tea Ceremony, as it was explained to me, could

almost be called an esthetic rite. Its observance gave a new appreciation of art and of the beauty in everyday life. One should withdraw occasionally from the bustle of daily routine. In a place of quiet and simplicity one should sit with a few friends and, in the act of sharing tea, contemplate the surrounding beauty. From this symposium one should return to life with the fresh eyes of a child. The curator of the museum would show me an old Tea Ceremony house.

It was a day in late summer; a cold rain dripped slowly on the fallen leaves. Mist hid the hills. It was one of those days when a change in the weather suddenly arrests time. A day out of season, stopping the monotonous count of summer days. Stopping, too, one's own summer routine so that, looking out on the gray skies, one says not only, "What time of year is it?" but, "What time of life am I in? Where am I? What am I doing?" It was a day for contemplation and a visit to a Tea Ceremony house.

Following the path, we brushed under low branches. And the rain, which had stepped quietly on the leaves, beat like a drum on our paper umbrellas.

"The Tea House," said our teacher, "must always be apart from the house. One should drop care and come away to it."

The path was green with moss and partly hidden by overhanging trees. We came rather quickly upon a small roofed gate and a sheltered bench.

"Here the guests wait until the host is ready. There are only five at the Tea Ceremony, never more."

A good number, I thought. If one talks to more than four people, it is an audience; and one cannot really think or exchange thoughts with an audience.

"And when the host is ready the guests come through this garden." It was not a garden in our sense. There were no formal flower beds and no flowers, only spears of bamboo, little pines, and an old stone lantern. And though each stone and tree had been carefully placed, the studied simplicity of the whole gave the garden an air of natural rather than artificial beauty. Walking over the path of stepping-stones, one felt in the heart of the woods.

"The stones must be freshly sprinkled with water," continued the curator, "and they are carefully chosen, all of them; for the water must not dry from them too quickly. On the other hand, they must not be too wet; they should have the wetness of a pear newly peeled." There was no host to sprinkle the steps for us, but the rain made them shine. Unevenly placed as they were, it was impossible to walk safely upon them without looking down and noticing their beauty.

When I looked up again we were in front of the house. The curator stopped by an old stone well. "You see, mossgrown on the outside, but inside the well is scrubbed clean, for cleanliness must go with beauty. Here the guests stop and prepare themselves to enter the house."

We stood in front of the simplest type of Japanese architecture: a low one-story house, thatched roof, wood beams, and paper walls.

"Here on this shelf in former times the Samurai left his sword. For there is peace inside the Tea House. The guest leaves all outside—his rank, his position, his pride." (Here unobtrusively I left my umbrella.)

"The door is low." He knelt on the sill. "And one enters on one's knees—for humility's sake—and inside—"

We knelt on the matted floor of a little room. "The Tea Room is not built of stone and brick, for stone and brick imprison one. It should not shut out nature but merely be a shelter in the midst of nature. The song of birds comes easily through these paper walls. (I heard the crickets in the garden as he spoke.) And though the room is simple, it is made in exact and satisfying proportions. The windows are not all of the same height, for variety is needed in beauty as well as order. And the house itself is made of the finest material, but the finish is severely plain." The beams of unpolished wood which framed the Tokonoma were smooth and gleaming, reminding me of my doll's box.

"And though the room is not decorated in your sense, there are always several things of rare beauty placed in it by the host: a hanging scroll containing a poem or a painting by a famous master, an artistic flower arrangement." The shadow of a branch outside the window trembled lightly on the wall.

"And as the host prepares for tea the guests watch with respect and appreciation, for there is beauty in the simplest and most common things: in the rhythmic motion of sweeping, in the fire, in the boiling water." He lifted up the matting, took out a panel from the floor, and showed us the ashes of a charcoal stove.

"And the guests take their tea, silently, in serenity of mind and body." He held up his hand as though cupping an imaginary bowl of tea.

"As they look into their tea-bowl they may consider the beauty of the glaze and the curve of the shape; or they may consider the gentle words and philosphy of the Tea-master to whom that tea-bowl once belonged; or, letting their thoughts go further as they see the vapor rise and melt into the air, they may consider the evanescence of life."

If only I could stay here long enough, I thought, going home in the rain, I would learn to see too. And after minutely watching the surface of things I would learn to see below the surface. I would see the essence of a thing, what it has in common with other things: that is, I would learn *simile*. I would see that a certain wet stone (as my Japanese friend said) was wet as a new-peeled pear. Then I would learn *metaphor* and see in my little boy "My hunter of the dragon fly." And finally I would learn *symbolism*. "The bamboo for prosperity," a Japanese friend explained to me, "the pine for long life, the plum for courage—"

"Why the plum for courage?" I asked, picturing courage as a great oak.

"Yes, yes," answered my Japanese friend. "The plum for courage, because the plum puts forth blossoms while the snow is still on the ground."

SIXTEEN

Stowaway

❈

We were on the wharf at Osaka, about to leave the main island of Japan. Our plane, which had been in the hangar during our excursions by car to Kyoto and Nara, was already wheeled out on its cradle and stood, its harness attached to the derrick, ready to be lowered into the water. In the hot summer sky over our heads, two or three planes zoomed in a farewell salute. We had shaken hands with the line of white-uniformed officials behind us, "Thank you, Thank you"—"Sayonara"; we had waved at our friends. We turned to go. The line of photographers set up their tripods and adjusted their cameras. I jumped on to the cradle and climbed up the side of the ship, my husband behind me, shoving our two blanket rolls of clothing ahead of him on to the wing. Everything else was packed up. Even the maps, the radio pads, and the lunches were tucked into a pocket in my cockpit.

My husband stood on the wing and opened the baggage-compartment door. He was reaching down to pick up one of our bundles when he noticed that the baggage was not as he left it. He always packed up the equipment himself and took great pride in the neat orderly way in which it all fitted down and presented an even surface which could be covered by the canvas flaps and strapped in place. (I was never allowed to touch it in case I should put the bag of emergency medicines or delicate instruments down underneath cans of tomatoes or the tool-kit.)

Someone had been meddling this time, he could see that. Not much was out of place, but the two canteens had been removed from their corner and sat untidily on top of all the other luggage. It annoyed him a little, as the officials had just explained carefully that no one had been allowed even to touch the plane in our absence. Still, it was not important. He lifted up the flap of canvas to put them back. There, fitted snugly in with the rest of the baggage, was a human head—a closely cropped dark head, face down. As far as he could see there was no body. There was not room for a body. Moving the canvas a little more, he could see the gray cloth of trousers—of knees—a man —stowaway. He turned and looked back at me. Without saying a word or showing the slightest consternation he motioned me to come forward. His face was a little serious. Gracious! I thought. What have I broken now!

"Look in there," he said quietly. I looked, felt my heart beat a little faster, and then whispered stupidly, "What—is it?" (Though it was quite obvious what it was.)

Just as quietly he asked one of the officials to come up. There was no doubt in the officer's mind. He pushed back a bundle and disclosed more gray coat. Stowaway! He called sharply to another official. Two came running. The expectant lull, which had fallen on the crowd prior to our taking off, broke into a confused murmur. And all the time the huddled form in the baggage compartment never stirred. By now there were at least three uniformed officers on the wing and many more under it looking up. There was a good deal of talking back and forth which we did not understand. Finally one of the officers called to the stowaway to come out. No movement. They reached in and began to pull him. It was the scene in *Alice in Wonderland*

reversed: the Dormouse being pulled out of the teapot
—a difficult process.

The Dormouse, who was rather a good-sized boy
of eighteen, was extremely stiff and cramped. He had
evidently climbed in the night before and had held
himself in this crunched-up position, his knees tightly
squeezed against his chest probably for many hours.
He had almost fitted himself into the space of two two-
gallon canteens. Yanked and pulled, he managed to get
out, a very dejected picture, his head lowered, his
gray cotton public-school uniform wet with perspi-
ration. It must have been stifling in the closed compartment. Under his arm was a large colored handkerchief,
knotted and rather soiled, in which (we learned later)
he had a few gumdrops. This was all he had taken with
him except for thirteen yen in his pockets. He never
looked up as he climbed out of the ship, but was half
carried down on to the dock and then shuffled off into
the hangar, an officer on each arm.

We asked them not to punish him too severely, for
he seemed a pathetic figure. He did not want to harm
anyone; he did not want publicity. He did not care
about flying or with whom he was going, they found
out from questioning. No, none of those things interested him. It was much simpler than that. He was, in
fact, a genuine stowaway, intent only on getting transportation. Life was not very happy at home. He had
read in the newspapers about this aviator who had
come from America—and would presumably go back
there. Here was his chance to escape. He would go to
America.

Ironically enough, we were headed toward China.

SEVENTEEN

A River

✿

Our first sign of China was indicative of the immensity of the country we were going to. It was an unexpected sign, for, flying over the Yellow Sea from Japan, we were looking for land on the horizon ahead, perhaps even the outline of mountains like the horizon behind us. But long before the darker blue of solid land began to rise above the shifting blue of the sea, China came out to meet us. We were aware of a difference in color between the water in front of us and the water behind us, a sharp line of demarcation where brown waves met blue. Mud from the Yangtze River darkened the sea for miles ahead. We were approaching China.

What a river this must be to make itself felt so far out from land, to so impress its personality on its over-lord, the sea. I made obeisance to it in my mind, for I felt in the presence of a great monarch. And I was not mistaken. The Yangtze River, as we followed its smooth course up through the immense stretches of flat farm land of coastal China, was one of those rivers which give the impression of being the only true and permanent rulers of the earth.

Rivers perhaps are the only physical features of the world that are at their best from the air. Mountain ranges, no longer seen in profile, dwarf to anthills; seas lose their horizons; lakes have no longer depth but look like bright pennies on the earth's surface; forests become a thin impermanent film, a moss on the top of a wet stone, easily rubbed off. But rivers, which from the ground one usually sees only in cross sections, like a small sample of ribbon—rivers stretch out serenely ahead as far as the eye can reach. Rivers are seen in their true stature.

They tumble down mountain sides; they meander

through flat farm lands. Valleys trail them; cities ride them; farms cling to them; roads and railroad tracks run after them—and they remain, permanent, possessive. Next to them, man's gleaming cement roads which he has built with such care look fragile as paper streamers thrown over the hills, easily blown away. Even the railroads seem only scratched in with a penknife. But rivers have carved their way over the earth's face for centuries and they will stay.

We have seen the Susquehanna cutting across the Allegheny ridges, and have followed the Mississippi, carrying half a continent of farms magnificently on its far-reaching banks. We have watched the Rio Grande ride like a plumed serpent through the sandy wastes of the Southwest (golden sand bars streaked with water, like feathers from the air); and the innocent trickle of the Colorado River, gleaming incongruously at the bottom of a gigantic crack in the earth's face. "That little silver thread made the Grand Canyon?" one asks. "Impossible!"

We have a great respect for rivers and usually they are kind to fliers. Sometimes it is just the exchange of a nod between travelers journeying over the same country. From Kansas City to St. Louis, there is the Missouri. It curls off in smooth circles to our right. We do not follow its course, but see it gleaming ahead in patches on the curves, like a skipping stone, coming up again and again. A line, a curve, a golden S, glinting, disappearing, glinting. What pleasure at rediscovery, like a recurring melody in music.

Sometimes, though, it is more than that. It is a hand in the dark. How many times, flying over nameless stretches in the West, some river has proved an incontestable landmark. "The Cimarron—good! We've crossed the line then—we're in Oklahoma—" And at night, when the whole universe seems a bowl of darkness uniformly starred top to bottom, gradually as one's eyes become accustomed to the dark there is that line, that demarcation, a difference in consistency in the

substance below—something that holds light, reflec-
tions—"a river—the Ohio!"

There are rivers that have cut a way for us through
a mountain ridge, tunnels under the fog that one can
pass through safely, like the Delaware Water Gap.
And there are nameless rivers, too, often too small to
be shown on our maps, that have led us over a pass in
the mountains. Following a ravine up one side of a
mountain range, a river below always there to lead us
back to the valley we have just left behind. Then for
a while we lose it and fight over a nameless territory,
lakes and forests on the top of a pass. And again we
pick up the silver trail, a river dashing over bowlders
in the opposite direction—west. We have crossed the
divide; we are over.

This time we were to see the river not as a friend,
but as an enemy; not at peace, but in revolt. We were
to see it in flood, destroying the fertile plains it had
once made, breaking dykes, carrying away villages,
and covering valleys. We were to see it, a huge lake
smiling catlike, horribly calm and complacent, over
the destroyed fields and homes of millions of people.
And again, an angry sea, its muddy waves battering
down houses; or a turbulent stream spouting through
a break in the dykes. And always in the center of the
wide area of destruction that roaring torrent, darker
and more turbulent than the rest, the very heart of
the river gone mad with power, carrying all in front
of it; houses, trees, boats, live stock, and coffins—inevitably swept along out to sea.

The yellow waters of the Yangtze surrounded our
short weeks in China. They led us into the country
and held us there in our attempt to chart the extent
of their damage. For our plane was the only one in
China which had enough range to survey the outer
limits of the floods. It was the Yangtze River we followed up and down its swollen course. And it was the
Yangtze River in the end which took us out of China.

EIGHTEEN

The Wall of Nanking

❀

The wall of Nanking is such a dominating feature of the city that it seems almost a geographical one. Fliers are apt to picture places in purely geographical terms. And as I remember our fleeting visit to Nanking, I see first a river, a mountain, and a wall.

The river takes precedence in my mind, for we followed its broad course for miles, ponderous, inevitable, ahead of us, our road to Nanking. It was also the road of innumerable other travelers below: big river boats chugging up the current; top-heavy junks with their square parchment-colored sails, webbed like a bat's wing; heavily loaded rafts, and even thin slivers of sampans—all marking a way to the crowded docks of Nanking.

The mountain rising east of Nanking I remember because it is typical of a new country that we approached after leaving the coastal plains of China. Those endless stretches of small fields disappear as one travels up the Yangtze and low hills climb from the horizon. "Purple Mountain," also, because of its height and sharpened peak, forms a landmark, visible to a flier long before the smoke of a city or the outline of a wall. As we came nearer, its gentle slopes seemed to be encroaching on the city, as the river encroached on the opposite side. One physical feature faces the other, vying in strength.

And between them stands the wall of Nanking, throwing its gray rope around hills and fields, railroads and canals, mud huts and tiled roofs, pointed eaves and towers, crowded streets and shaded gardens, drawing them all together into what is now the capital of China.

A walled city has an unmistakable quality of majesty. It stands isolated as an island, self-sufficient as a ship, unassailable as a mountain. It seems to have all the attributes of a monarch. And looked at from the air, the city of Nanking does wear its wall like a crown.

From the ground one is still more conscious of its majesty, looking up at the crenelated outline, or passing under the massive gates. For the traffic of Nanking, jostling down the narrow streets, still threads through needle-eye gates. A bustling line of rickshaws, the ragged blue coats of the runners flapping in the breeze; long-gowned men and women; venders, balancing from their shoulder poles the weight of stove and food basket; workmen, in harsh blue coats, and trousers rolled halfway up their bare legs, carrying three or four bags of flour on their shoulders; small high Cinderella-pumpkin coaches; squeaking wheelbarrows; a boy trying to sell two small fish squeezed in his fist; a woman with a few branches of sweet-smelling wild olive—all making their way over the cobblestoned street to one of the peak-roofed gates of the Nanking wall.

It was the eastern gate we passed under on our way to the plane. We had landed in Lotus Lake, just outside the city. The flooded waters stretched to the foot of the wall, like a medieval moat. Willows stood knee-deep on the edges, trailing their branches in the water, and sampans pressed down the submerged grass. Here we anchored our plane and came each morning to begin our survey flights. Here we left it each night, its orange wings still catching the light from an evening sky.

In the morning the wall was gray and hard, every brick standing out in its hardness. But in the evening, shadows from the moss and vines growing in the cracks gave it a purplish bloom, as though it caught some reflection from the opposite mountain. Massive as a mountain, too, it stood there in the twilight. The plane in front of it, glistening and sleek, swayed gently in the wind. It seemed to me as I watched, one against the other, that there was an argument between the two. Not only the perpetual argument of youth against age, but machine-made against man-made; things fleeting against things lasting; motion against rest; ambition against acceptance. It was an argument without end. I do not know who won, but as we poled home in the shadows, I could imagine it echoing back and forth:

"I am a wall. Generations have passed under my gates; wars and destruction have broken over me like waves. I am still here—a wall."

"I am a plane. Power and speed. I traverse space and race with time. You are bound; but I can fly—I am a plane."

"I am a wall. You are a plane; you will be gone to-morrow. But I—I will be here forever—a wall."

". . . a plane . . ."

". . . a wall. . . ."

NINETEEN
The Floods

❀

Before we left Japan we knew that the lower Yangtze valley was badly flooded. But we had no picture in our minds of the size or character of this valley. Only someone who has been there can imagine the amount of damage a flood can do.

Looking down on it from the air on our flight to Nanking, we saw that there was nothing to stop a flood. Flat fields for miles and miles—and the great massive river. The impression of magnificence is perhaps similar from any great river and its valley. And yet if one compares this yellow river to the Mississippi, one is aware of a vast difference. The Yangtze valley, despite the immense expanse of land, still seems crowded. Every inch of ground is cultivated, not in big tracts, like our farms, but in narrow strips of rice fields, slivering off at right angles to the river. No wild land, no forests; just thin back-yard strips of field with occasionally a crowded village of mud huts, representing thousands of people.

One did not have to be told that this was a land in which there could be no waste; that people here lived literally from day to day; that there was no "extra" stored away; that even the shucks of the crop and the dry grass were saved for fuel, because the trees had gone long ago.

This was the type of country into which the floods came, destroying crops, homes, and people. And this was the type of country over which we did most of our survey flying. For on our arrival in Nanking we offered to help the National Flood Relief Commission by mapping the damaged areas.

On the first day's flight we left our anchorage at Lotus Lake in the morning and for a time followed the river east until it met the Grand Canal, then turned and flew north. At first we noticed only the obviously flooded fields along the banks of the river, the green of late crops showing through the water. Then gradually we became aware of a number of "lakes" which constantly increased until finally they gave the impression of one big lake, enormous, stretching as far as we could see. I realized with a shock that this was not "lake"; it was all flood. Yet it did not have the look of fields covered with water. Deep and wide, horribly still and permanent, it looked as though it had always been there and would always stay. (There was in fact no hope of its going down before spring, and this was early fall.)

Flying lower we could see suggestions of what the land was like under the flood: fields under water; hundreds of small villages standing in water, many of them up to their roofs; towns whose dykes and walls had given way, whose streets were canals; in some places, nothing but the tops of a few trees, with here and there a smear of brown on the surface, where a dyke or a road or a mud village had once been. In this last territory one dared not think how many lives had been lost. There was no trace left. In less badly flooded country the people had built up temporary mud dykes around their villages and pulled inside their first crop. But it was a hopeless fight. For these hastily slapped-up walls, guarding a group of huts and a rescued grain stack, were rapidly crumbling before the constant lapping of little waves, whipped up by the wind.

There was no dry land for miles around. Most of the people who were near enough to the border to escape had crowded into the outlying cities. Thousands of refugees had put up temporary grass shelters along the dykes lining the Grand Canal and on an uncompleted road just south of the flooded area. But there were thousands more who would never get out, who, their homes completely destroyed, were living in flat-bottomed sampans, with a grass roof rigged up in one end for shelter. Moored in the old streets or floating about the flooded fields, these refugees were apparently living only on the few straws of grain they had saved and what fish they might catch.

The small sampan driven by oar or pole seemed to be the only possible means of transportation in this vast area. Looking down on them, myriads of gnats on the surface of the water, we began to realize the hopelessness of the situation. How could relief ever reach these people? The water was not deep enough for large boats. There were no roads and probably never had been. There were almost no large centers from which food could be distributed, just thousands of small isolated villages—or what remained of them—stretched out over an area larger than Massachusetts.

Some things could be and were being done by the

Relief Commission. Food could be taken to the refugee camps in or near the few larger centers, and, what was even more needed, medical supplies and assistance to stop the epidemics which inevitably follow a flood. We could not help to carry food, as the weight would be prohibitive in a plane; but we could perhaps carry medical supplies and a doctor.

My husband was trying to do this the day he set out for Hinghwa. We had seen the walled city from the air on our first day's flight. It was marooned in the center of a large flooded area; the nearest dry ground was more than twenty-five miles to the south. Medical aid, the Commission felt, was probably as badly needed there as anywhere, and it would be a good center for distribution. So one morning my husband took off from Nanking, carrying with him in the plane a Chinese doctor, an American doctor, and several packages of medical supplies. I had given up my place to one doctor. The baggage compartment had been cleared of much emergency equipment to lighten the load and make room for the second.

In less than an hour they completed a trip which would have taken days by canal. The plane landed on flooded fields outside the city walls. A few stray sampans were the only signs of life on the calm waters. The Chinese doctor, who was to land with supplies, waved at them and finally persuaded one boat to pull up alongside. Others straggled behind curiously. Slowly the doctor climbed down out of the cockpit and stepped from the pontoon into the sampan. Carefully a package of medicines was handed down after him. An old woman took it in her arms, put it down on the floor of the sampan, and sat on it firmly.

There was a stir of curiosity in the surrounding boats. By now there were ten or twenty of them poling about. Men, women, and children, sullen and hungry, looked at the package and began to murmur among themselves. "Food," they were saying, "there must be food in the box." They pushed forward and soon surrounded the doctor's boat as it poled out. Others pressed nearer the plane.

My husband stood up in the cockpit and motioned them back. (One of the heavy prows could easily knock a hole in our pontoons.) But they paid no attention to him. And there were more sampans coming every minute, attracted by the strange craft. They sprang up from nowhere like flies on a summer day. The American doctor began to shout to them in Chinese, telling them to keep back. But the starving people were thinking only of one thing. They made cups out of their hands and pretended to be eating with chopsticks. "The foreigners must understand now; we want food." The word spread like fire leaping across a field in a high wind. It reached the outer circle of boats, and people began jumping from one boat to another toward the plane. For they could no longer pole any nearer. There were literally hundreds of sampans now, boat jammed against boat on all sides. The nearest were right under the wings and tail surfaces. A sampan under the left wing had a small fire dangerously near its grass hood. Shouting, either in English or Chinese, had no effect and—worse still—there were even more coming. In the distance one could see a solid stream of boats rounding the city wall.

"Have you a gun?" the American doctor shouted.

"Yes—" said my husband, "a thirty-eight revolver—but someone in that crowd"—looking out at thousands of sullen and desperate faces—"may have a rifle—probably several—fatal to show a gun in a crowd like that."

Nevertheless he hid it under his parachute, planning not to use it unless they started to board the plane. People were hanging on to wings, pontoons, and tail surfaces but no one had yet actually tried to climb on.

Suddenly a man stood up and put his foot on the left pontoon. As though at a signal the rest surged forward. Now a man was on the other pontoon. They had begun to board.

My husband grabbed his revolver and covered the nearest man. He stopped but did not move back. My husband turned to the right side. Those faced with the gun hesitated, but the men on the other side moved up. He whipped the gun from the right side to the left quickly, shooting straight up in the air as he turned. Each side thought someone had been shot on the other. He moved it back and forth quickly, covering always the nearest person. Slowly they edged back.

The two men in the plane stopped to breathe and to look for the Chinese doctor. He had completely lost track of the package soon after leaving the plane. It had been seized from his sampan and fought over as a crust of bread is torn apart by gulls. His own boat, overloaded with men who had jumped in from other sampans, had sunk under the weight. With the water curling over the edges, he stepped quickly into another. The crowd followed him, thinking where he went the package would eventually go too. Three boats sank under him. In the middle of an island of sampans, people fighting and pushing around him, he knew there was no hope of rescuing the vaccines or of reaching the city. He hoped he could get back to the plane alive. Finally, arguing with a boatload that there was a larger package in the plane, he managed to reach the front ring of sampans only to be faced with a pistol! He stood up and shouted excitedly before he was recognized. In the cleared space in front of him, he was able to reach the plane and climbed hurriedly into the back cockpit.

The American doctor in the meantime was hauling up the anchor as fast as he could. There was no time to stow it in the pontoon anchor-hatch, where it usually fitted in the neat coils of rope. He stuffed it, rope and all, in the baggage compartment, and started to climb in on top. They were clear, ready to go.

No—there was a single sampan just in front of the plane, an old man and an old woman poling it. My

husband raised himself up in the cockpit and covered
them with his gun. The American doctor jumped out
on the wing and shouted, "Get out of the way! We'll
kill you!"

They made no move. The old woman looked up
sullenly, "What does it matter?" she said slowly. "We
have nothing."

The plane swung slightly in the wind, pointing clear
of the sampan. My husband pressed the starter. The
engine caught—an answering roar. They took off dead
ahead, over flooded fields, between fences, collapsed
roofs, and grave-mounds, regardless of wind direction
—anything to get off, to shake that trailing wake of
hundreds of sampans, those arms paddling as fast as
they could in a vain attempt to follow.

The plane left the water, rising easily, roaring up-
wards in one wide circle. Men, boats, fields, and huts
dropped off below the wing and were left behind. In
a few seconds it was high above that flooded world.
The milling mass of sampans was a swarm of gnats
on the water's surface. Even the city of Hinghwa (from
whose gates boats were still streaming) looked insignificant, a small island of roofs in the vast sea of flood
that surrounded it.

Looking down on the spot they had just left, the
men in the plane were acutely conscious of the miracle of their escape. A moment before they had been
down in that crowd of starving people, some of whom
might live until spring; many would die before the
waters receded. Now, headed for Nanking, safety,
food, and shelter were as assured to the fliers as in their
own homes. Separated from those desperate people
below only by a few seconds in time, only by a few
hundred feet in distance, they were yet irretrievably
removed in some fourth dimension. The two worlds
were separated by a gulf which, although not wide,
was deep, perilous, and unbridgeable. At least it was
unbridgeable to the owners of the sampans. The fliers

had crossed over from one world to another as easily, as swiftly, as one crosses from the world of nightmare to the world of reality in the flash of waking.

They had a gun; they had a plane—powerful as any genii to be summoned from a magic lamp. And yet, magic rests on a knife-edge—a lamp, a tinder-box, an "open sesame." It is a hair-bridge between captivity and escape; safety and danger; life and death. The pull of a trigger, the press of a switch—without these, the three magicians flying back to Nanking would have been simply three people in a starving, dying, and devastated land.

TWENTY

The Most Beautiful Pagoda

✲

"By the way," he said, half speaking to himself, half to us, "the most beautiful pagoda in China is down in that region." He spoke lightly and dismissed quickly from our minds the picture he had drawn. It was a lapse into another world, a world we had not time to think about then. We were talking about the floods. The group of men who were investigating the flooded areas, supervising the aid that was to be given, were seated around a table in Nanking, going over maps with my husband. Where was survey most needed? How far did the waters reach in that direction? How badly flooded was that valley? These were the important questions.

So I never asked about the pagoda, and never really thought about it again, though the phrase remained in the back of my mind like the beginning of a fairy

tale: "The most beautiful Princess in the kingdom . . ."

I did not think about it until one day we found it.
I do not know—in fact, it was probably not the pagoda
our friend was speaking of. But that does not matter.
It was "the most beautiful pagoda in China," I am sure
of that.

It was at the end of the day. We had flown to the
limits of the flood and were now out in wilder land,
above a circle of hills. And there it was. In this circle
there was a lake. And on this lake there was an island;
and on this island there was a pagoda. There it was,
just like the fairy tale. Even the landscape seemed unreal, for in that late afternoon mist the hills and islands
looked as they do in some of the old oriental scroll
paintings—not placed according to the conventions of
perspective, one behind another, but as though each
were suspended, one above the other in some atmos-
phere, some wash all of the same tone.

The pagoda would have been beautiful by virtue
of its setting alone, ringed as it was three times by
land and water and land—a triple ring that gave it an
air of an enchanted pagoda, safely imprisoned there
by some wizard's decree. Centered like that, a gem in
its frame, it gave one also an indescribable feeling of
finality and peace, as though one had reached the end
of the journey or come to the heart of some mystery.
Its setting, also, intensified the impression of aloneness.
Ringed by silence, the pagoda was. And the things
that are alone and ringed by silence must be beautiful.
It is James Stephens' poem:

> Under a lonely sky a lonely tree
> Is beautiful! All that is loneliness
> Is beautiful.

And yet it was not only beautiful for its setting. It
was beautiful in its very structure; one curved roof on
another in a gently tapering tower—sloping roofs with

petal-like eaves pointing upward, like the drooping bell of a lily. So that one's eye, although drawn inevitably upward, still retained the impression of those downward-sloping roofs. And the pleasure at the sight was the same as from listening to those climbing songs that rise and fall and rise again to a new height, the same figure repeated over again at a new peak. So the pagoda, although it was the embodiment of all peace and stillness, at the same time suggested growth.

It was—as I have said—the most beautiful pagoda in China.

We flew around it three times and went away.

One night in New York, several years after our return, a traveler from the East was talking about China. I could hardly follow his words, that hot evening, through the complaints of taxi horns pressing in the wide-open windows, when suddenly I was listening as one listens, pricked by a name, across a room full of conversation, to someone talking in the opposite corner.

He was speaking. about the pagoda. I recognized it not so much from the description as from the story he told. A story which rang with a truth as compelling as those forgotten tunes which suddenly sing in the mind. One stands still in front of them, waiting with terror and delight, as they dance toward one. For they cannot be forced. And an eager step forward may frighten them away.

"And the pagoda," he continued, "is so beautiful that once a year all the other pagodas in China make a journey there, and bow down before it, on their knees."

TWENTY-ONE

Into the Yangtze

✷

It was to be our last flight over the flooded areas. The British airplane carrier *Hermes* was leaving in the morning and we with it. For it had been our home at Hankow. When we arrived, two or three days before, we hoped to anchor in a sheltered bend of the river or in a lake or flooded field. But there were no lakes, and the floods immediately around the city had subsided too much for us to land over fields. The river, although still swollen, and dangerously swift and turbulent, was the only place to anchor. Here we came down and taxied up to the *Hermes*, mooring first to a long rope trailed from its stern. But the plane, although securely tied, swung from side to side in the current, right in the path of the Chinese junks which came down the river. Fearing it would be rammed at night, the captain of the *Hermes* offered to take the *Sirius* on board, hoisting it up from the water with harness and tackle as they did their own seaplanes.

We were extremely grateful. Not only was it unprecedented for a British carrier to take a foreign plane on board, but it meant additional work. Their harness would not fit our plane and they had to construct a new one. There was no time to make the regular quick-release mechanism for this. Instead, it had only a large steel ring which could be hooked up to the derrick. To release the plane after it was lowered into the water, the ring was simply lifted off the hook. But this could not be done without three or four inches of slack in the cable.

When we were first hoisted aboard, everything went well. There was plenty of time, as we taxied slowly upstream and under the derrick, for the mechanics to fit ring to hook. Fortunately there was scarcely any wind to add to our difficulties. By using the motor we were able to keep motionless against the current. Even so, one wing-tip dipped into the water, caught for a second, then slipped free as the derrick raised us.

Those few seconds made us see, though it was just the unconscious stirring of a giant in his sleep, what power for destruction lay in the current and how completely we were at its mercy. We realized then the chance we were taking every time we raised or lowered our plane. But it was an emergency. The flights would have to be made that way or not at all. Most of the work was now done. The British planes had covered all of the territory around Hankow and we had reached the outer limits of the floods except for one area.

It was, as I have said, our last flight. But it was to be the first one for the Chinese doctor. Our passenger for the day, he was to ride in the baggage compartment. As he could not swim we decided not to take him aboard until the plane was safely lowered. He sat and waited in a small boat near the stern of the carrier. My husband and I climbed into our cockpits while the *Sirius* was still on deck. A mechanic stood on each wing. Both wore life preservers, for the Yangtze has a bad reputation. "No one," we were told in Hankow, "who goes under its yellow surface, ever comes up again."

The plane teetered forward slightly as the derrick started to hoist us. Several men hung on to the pontoons to steady us as we swung free. Now we were above their heads; and now gliding over the rail to the water below. It seemed rather abnormal and a little perilous to be sailing quietly through the air, not propelled by our own power. I felt relieved when finally, after a slow descent, we touched the water. Headed upstream, the idling motor now quickened to a roar, we seemed safely launched. The men started to lift the ring of our harness from the derrick hook.

"Let it out there—more slack!" Shouts from plane

to ship. One man was clinging to the cable with all his weight. The second wrestled with ring and hook.

"No slack—can't do it!" We were drifting rapidly further from the ship, the cable already taut. My husband, opening the throttle, tried to work back upstream. But the plane had already swung in the wind sidewise to the current. We were only pulling away from the carrier. The cable stretched tauter. He closed the throttle, and cut the switch. No use. We turned still more to the side. Out of control. Current pulled against cable. Something had to go.

Down went the wing. Its tip touched the water and went under, an enormous paddle, with the current eddying up on one side. It acted like a paddle too, that large flat surface stemming the stream, forcing us over.

"Better get ready to jump!" My husband's voice shot at me tersely from the front cockpit. I climbed out. Nothing could save us now. We were already at an angle, and turning fast.

"Jump!"

I looked down into the muddy current. In that fleeting second preparatory to action, that second of winding up the springs, I thought only, with incongruous complacency, "Now I will find out how this new life preserver works." (It was supposed to inflate when one pressed a lever.) I pushed the lever and jumped. The wing darkened above me as I went under. I remember thinking, clearly, calmly, without a trace of fear, as though watching some event outside myself, "I suppose that wing may hit me as it falls over." It did not worry me. I was simply interested in weighing the chances, just as one might say in a sailboat, judging quickly with one's eye, "I don't think I'll make the buoy on this tack." It was a matter of fact and not of feeling.

For not only did I have no fear, I had no sensation at all—no realization of going under water or of getting wet or of my clothes being heavy to swim in, or even that the life preserver had not worked. Quite typically I had not pressed the lever far enough. It did not matter. I had come up and was swimming along easily with yards of deflated life preserver dragging after me. Looking around quickly, I saw my husband just behind. The two men from the *Hermes* were alongside of us. We were swept downstream to the lifeboat, where we climbed on board and wiped our faces. I coughed up some Yangtze water. "And for three weeks," I thought, "I've been brushing my teeth in boiled water!"

But the plane—we turned and looked back. It was upside down, still held by the derrick cable, one wing and the tail submerged. The steel harness had cut through the plywood on top of the fuselage as it turned over. Bits of covering and broken plywood were tearing away from the submerged wing, streaming down past our boat. For one sickening moment I thought the *Sirius* was going to pieces before our eyes. It was in the grip of a mad force, tireless, unceasing, and irresistible, which would devour it as fire devours a frame house. All the infinite care that goes to make up a plane, the smooth fashioning of the wood for the wings, the delicate precision of the machinery for the engine; and all our work, the whole summer—everything was to be lost in a few seconds in the destruction of the *Sirius*. It was no more than a little match box crushed in a giant's hand. The river seemed to me wantonly destructive, pitting all its strength against us to no purpose. I became acutely conscious of the immorality of that force at work in the waves, eagerly tearing down well-built structure. Why does it work so hard merely to destroy?

The plane, however, was standing up surprisingly well in the fight. There was a hole in the fuselage and several in one wing but apparently no important damage had yet been done. It might still be saved, righted with ropes and then hoisted up on deck again. My husband went back in the launch and climbed up the fuselage to the high wing. Ignoring, like a disagreeable little boy on the roof, all shouts of "Come down off there!" he managed to fasten ropes to the wing and propeller. A launch from the American gunboat was to right the plane by pulling a rope attached to the free wing. A second rope from the propeller to the *Hermes* held the nose pointed upstream. With the plane now steadied from three different directions, the launch began to pull.

Just as the cable tautened, down the river came a sampan full of Chinese. They were headed straight for the launch. A stroke or two in the right direction could carry them safely clear of it. There was still plenty of time. A stroke in the wrong direction would head them into the rope. Could they get under before the plane turned? No, it would flip over just as they arrived. The rope slapping across the water would spill the whole craft into the current. And they would never come up again. Most Chinese cannot swim.

"For God's sake, stop them!" Yells of warning. Men waved frantically. The commander stood up and shouted futilely through his megaphone.

The boatload was obviously confused. There was an argument going on. Which way would they go? Arms waved in the air. In the meantime the current was carrying them nearer. All at once someone made the wrong stroke. It was decided. They were headed straight for the cable, inevitably swept along into the trap. The plane balanced for a second, one wing high in the air. Under the rope they skimmed, still gesticulating. The plane quivered, leaned to one side and fell heavily. The rope lashed across the water just behind the sampan. They escaped.

That evening when we sat talking the day over, I thought about the boatload of Chinese. Did they feel as relieved as I at escape from danger?

"They feel much happier," I was told. "They have cut all three devils off behind them."

"Three devils?"

"Yes," explained our friend. "Many Chinese believe

they are followed by three devils. If they can jump in front of a car and have it skim by, just missing the back of their heels, it is a great piece of luck."

"But why?"

"Well, you see," he continued, "the car has sliced between them and the devils, breaking the chain. Of course, if the car is further behind, it may only catch one devil."

He smiled, "There wasn't any doubt about it today, though—they lost all three."

TWENTY-TWO

"Sayonara"

✦

"Sayonara, Sayonara!" I was in my stateroom but I could hear them, outside on the deck of the Japanese boat, calling to friends and relatives on the dock at Shanghai. "Sayonara"—up and down the gangplank and over the rails. A boatload of Japanese were leaving China for home, as we were. "Sayonara," the chains clanked and the warning whistle shook the boat. The voices outside rose in a flurry of noise, like a flock of frightened birds. But above the conglomerate sound there was always one voice, clean and sharp and individual and yet representative of the mass like that one face in the front line that holds the meaning of the whole crowd—one cry, "Sayonara." The impression was intensified perhaps because it was the one word of Japanese I understood—"Sayonara" ("Good-by").

I was to hear it again, all along our trip home. For we crossed Japan by train from the southern tip to Yokohama, where we boarded the boat for America.

"Sayonara": the clatter of wooden clogs along the

station platform; the flutter of kimonos; babies jogging on their mothers' backs; men carrying four or five small bundles tied up in different-colored furoshiki (squares of parti-colored silk or cotton); old women knocking along with their sticks, their brown faces hidden under enormous rooflike hats of straw; a man shouting his wares. We leaned out of the window at one of these stations and motioned to a vender for some tea. He poured out of his big tin into a little brown clay teapot like a child's toy, with a saucer for a lid and an inverted cup on top. "Two! Two!" we shouted and signaled as the train jerked forward, starting to pull out. The vender ran after us with another teapot swinging from its wire handle and pushed it in our window.

"Sayonara—Sayonara!" cried the passengers who had just stepped on board. A Japanese family across the aisle from us leaned out of the window to say a few last words. They occupied two long seats raised on a slight platform, separated from the next family by a partition. The mother and nurse (or older sister) were dressed in Japanese kimonos, the father in Western business suit, the two little girls in green challis suits with Irish-lace collars, and the baby in woolens. They had already kicked off their shoes, in Japanese fashion, and were squatting on their feet on the blue plush seats. They held the baby up to the window for the last good-by—"Sayonara"; and then the monotonous doggerel rhythm of the train, quickening to a roar, drowned all noise. We were off.

It was good-by for us too, as we rushed through Japan on our way to the boat. Good-by to the rice fields terraced up a narrow gully in the hills; to thatched roofs and paper walls; to heavy-headed grain bent to a curve; to a field of awkward lotus leaves, like big elephant ears, flapping on their tall stalks; to a white road leading up a hill to a pine grove and the flicker of red of a shrine gate. Good-by to the little towns we rattled through, with their narrow cobbled streets lined

with shops, open to the passer-by except for fluttering
blue-toweling curtains or bright paper and cloth flag-
signs. Good-by to blue paper umbrellas in the rain and
little boys chasing dragon flies.

Our real good-by was not until the boat pulled out of
the dock at Yokohama, when the crowd of Japanese
leaning over the rails of the decks shot twirling strands
of serpentine across to those they had left behind on
shore—a rain of bright fireworks. One end of these
colored paper ribbons was held in the hands of those
on deck, the other, by those on shore, until a brilliant
multicolored web was spun between ship and shore.
This and the shouts of conversation, unintelligible to
me, interlacing back and forth across the gap, made
up a finely woven band—a tissue, intricately patterned
and rich in texture which held together for a few more
seconds those remaining and those departing. Then the
gap of water slowly widening between dock and ship,
the ribbons tautened and snapped, the broken and
raveled ends twirling off idly into the water, floating
away with the unfinished ends of sentences. And nothing could bridge the gap but "Sayonara!"

For *Sayonara*, literally translated, "Since it must be
so," of all the good-bys I have heard is the most beautiful. Unlike the *Auf Wiedersehens* and *Au revoirs*, it
does not try to cheat itself by any bravado "Till we
meet again," any sedative to postpone the pain of sep-
aration. It does not evade the issue like the sturdy
blinking *Farewell*. *Farewell* is a father's *good-by*. It is—
"Go out in the world and do well, my son." It is encour-
agement and admonition. It is hope and faith. But it
passes over the significance of the moment; of parting it
says nothing. It hides its emotion. It says too little.
While *Good-by* ("God be with you") and *Adios* say
too much. They try to bridge the distance, almost to
deny it. *Good-by* is a prayer, a ringing cry. "You must
not go—I cannot bear to have you go! But you shall not
go alone, unwatched. God will be with you. God's hand
will be over you" and even—underneath, hidden, but

it is there, incorrigible—"I will be with you; I will watch you—always." It is a mother's *good-by*. But *Sayonara* says neither too much nor too little. It is a simple acceptance of fact. All understanding of life lies in its limits. All emotion, smoldering, is banked up behind it. But it says nothing. It is really the unspoken good-by, the pressure of a hand, "Sayonara."

TWENTY-THREE

Flying Again

❁

We were flying again, several years after our trip to the Orient. It was not a long flight nor an important one. It was not even particularly beautiful, just a casual trip from New York to Washington. We were not pressed for time; the weather was good; I had no radio to operate, no maps to look at. It was for me, simply flying, divorced from its usual accompanying responsibilities and associations. I could sit quite still and let the roar of the engine cover me like music. Throbbing with small monotone patterns, the vibration hummed in the soles of my feet, in the hollow of my back. It absorbed some restless side of me, and was satisfying as a hearth fire or rain on the roof. Contented, I could look down at that calm clear world below.

A new world, too, it was, for I had not flown in many months and the objects below me wore the freshly painted vividness of things seen for the first time. They passed, bright and irrelevant images, slowly under the still suspended wheel of our plane. (A wooded hill like moss, soft gray moss to crush in one's hand. The shadow of a single elm, flat on the ground, like a pressed fern. Pointed cedars and their shadows, two pronged forks—for, in this world of flat surfaces, shadows are of equal importance with their objects. Pools in the fields as though the earth had just risen from the flood, shaking its shoulders. The sides of houses, hit by the morning sun, bright rectangles and squares, like the facets of cut stones.)

My eye, unaccustomed, temporarily, to such vast expanses to graze on, nibbled first here and then there at the scenes below, not finishing one patch in orderly fashion before starting on a new one. The images that attracted me were unrelated and scattered, not strung along one thread by a road, not cupped within the rim of a lake. (The pencil-marked shadows of telegraph poles. The neatly combed fields. Docks and piers and bridges, flat slabs laid on the edge of a mirror. Birds, particles of sand floating gently down the air. Cities, sudden flashes from an apartment window or a moving car—strange that the flash should reach such a distance, like a bright speck of glass in a road, sparkling far beyond its worth.)

There was no limit to what the eye could seize or what the mind hold—no limit, except that somewhat blurred but inescapable line of the horizon ahead. And even that line looked as though it might be limitless also. For if one swept the eye swiftly through the compass of the sky, one could see, or thought one saw, that slightly bowed look to the earth's surface. If I could turn quickly enough, I felt, I would catch sight of those flat fields and blue hills slipping down the side of the round world.

But still, I did not need to; there was too much to see as it was. A clear and perfect morning except for a slight ground haze, perceptible only in the distance, which, hanging over the earth, made a second horizon above the first one—as though the world were sunk under water, slowly emerging as the morning wore on.

Here below me I was not conscious of the morning haze. Through depths of clear transparent air, I looked down and saw those myriad bright shells on the floor of the sea. (Buoys newly painted and drying on a

dock were scarlet lobster claws. Pierheads were pegs
in the mud.) For the objects scattered below me bore
no resemblance to those I had been living with. They
bore no relation to life. Rootless and impermanent, they
seemed strewn there accidentally, washed up carelessly
by some great tide of the sea; and left, limp, shining,
detached, for me to pick up and arrange in what patterns I might choose.

They did, in fact, already form patterns (that strange
blocklike pattern the rows of tenements made, doubled with their shadows; and the circular one of those
black cars all centering to one point like an anthill), but
they were new and different ones. They were patterns
which seemed trivial and aimless from this great height,
like the wavering, vinelike tracks crabs make in the
sand. (How slowly those little cars crawl along the
narrow ribbon paths!) And looking down on those little houses, those little paths, the narrow lines of black
beetles, the anthill traffic of cars, one sat back and wondered, "Why? What do we do this for? Why isn't life
simple and still and quiet? Was I really there yesterday? What was I doing?"

One could sit still and look at life from the air; that
was it. And I was conscious again of the fundamental
magic of flying, a miracle that has nothing to do with
any of its practical purposes—purposes of speed, accessibility, and convenience—and will not change as
they change. It is a magic that has more kinship with
what one experiences standing in front of serene ma-
donnas or listening to cool chorales, or even reading
one of those clear passages in a book—so clear and so
illuminating that one feels the writer has given the
reader a glass-bottomed bucket with which to look
through the ruffled surface of life far down to that still
permanent world below.

For not only is life put in new patterns from the air,
but it is somehow arrested, frozen into form. (The
leaping hare is caught in a marble panel.) A glaze is
put over life. There is no flaw, no crack in the surface;

a still reservoir, no ripple on its face. Looking down from the air that morning, I felt that stillness rested like a light over the earth. The waterfalls seemed frozen solid; the tops of the trees were still; the river hardly stirred, a serpent gently moving under its shimmering skin. Everything was quiet: fields and trees and houses. What motion there was, took on a slow grace: the crawling cars, the rippling skin of the river, and birds drifting like petals down the air; like slow-motion pictures which catch the moment of outstretched beauty—a horse at the top of a jump—that one cannot see in life itself, so swiftly does it move.

And if flying, like a glass-bottomed bucket, can give you that vision, that seeing eye, which peers down to the still world below the choppy waves—it will always remain magic.

Appendix

Emergency Equipment for Forced Landing on Land
(Orient Flight—1931)

   1 revolver (38 cal.)
   1 revolver (22 cal.) (Listed under Emergency Equipment
      for Parachute Jump)
   1 gun-cleaning kit
 30 rounds 38 cal. ammunition
150 rounds 22 cal. ammunition
   1 bottle cleaning fluid
   1 hatchet
   1 machete
   1 Primus stove
   1 sheath knife
   1 compass (Listed under Emergency Equipment for Par-
      achute Jump)
   1 aluminum jar of matches
   1 tent (cloth floor and net door and windows)
   1 fish net (about 25 ft.) (Listed under Emergency
      Equipment for Parachute Jump)
    fishline
   3 spoon hooks
   9 plain hooks
   6 swivels
   2 gut cords
    sinkers to be obtained from engine if necessary (nuts,
      bolts, etc.)
   1 first-aid and medicine kit
   1 bottle quinine
    snake serum and syringe
    morphine
   2 mosquito head nets (Listed under Emergency Equip-
      ment for Parachute Jump)

2 blankets (used also to roll personal clothing in to save weight of suitcase) (Listed under Personal Equipment)
1 poncho
1 raincoat
1 sleeping bag
parachutes to be used for additional blankets if necessary (Listed under Emergency Equipment for Parachute Jump)
2 pr. high boots
1 aluminum frying pan
1 aluminum pot
cord (to be obtained from parachute shroud lines if necessary)
2 suits heavy wool underwear
wool socks (Listed under Personal Flying Equipment)
mittens (Listed under Personal Flying Equipment)
caps—helmets to be used for caps (Listed under Personal Flying Equipment)
scarfs—to be cut from parachutes in emergency
coats—to be cut from flying suits in emergency
other clothing (Listed under Personal Equipment)
portable radio set (Listed under Radio Equipment)
food and water (Listed under Emergency Food Provisions)
battery and generator flashlights (Listed under Navigation Equipment)

Emergency Equipment for Forced Landing at Sea
(Orient Flight—1931)

1 rubber boat
1 mast (in sections)
1 pr. oars
1 sail
1 boom
1 cross board for mast
1 rubber storm top for boat
2 air pumps
1 rubber patch kit (including rubber patch sheet and tube of cement)

  2 Armburst cups
    sextant, chronometers, and navigation equipment
      (Listed under Navigation Equipment)
    provisions (Listed under Emergency Food Provisions)
    water (Listed under Emergency Food Provisions)
    radio set (Listed under Radio Equipment)
    clothing (Listed under Personal Flying Equipment,
      Personal Equipment, Emergency Equipment for
      Forced Landing on Land)
  1 Very pistol
 10 cartridges (red)
  1 hatchet (Listed under Emergency Equipment for
    Forced Landing on Land)

        Emergency Equipment for Parachute Jump
              (Orient Flight—1931)

  2 seat-type silk parachutes
  1 canvas belt pouch
  1 one-quart canteen of water with shoulder strap
  1 revolver (22 cal.)
 50 rounds 22 cal. ammunition
    small first-aid and medicine kit
  1 compass
  1 pocket knife
  2 tins army rations (8 oz. each)
  1 match box and matches
  1 fish net (about 25 ft.)
  1 fishline
    fishhooks, swivels, and guts
    small coil flexible wire
  2 mosquito head nets

          Emergency Food Provisions
              (Orient Flight—1931)

  1 box hardtack
  8 pkgs. dried soup
  1 cheese
  2 cans powdered milk

   1 aluminum jar containing figs packed in rice
   6 cans tomatoes
   5 cans baked beans
   2 cans bouillon cubes
   1 can corned beef
   1 can tongue
   1 box prunes
   1 can crackers
   1 aluminum jar packed with dried beans, rice, and sugar
   1 aluminum jar containing dried soup packages
   1 container of salt
  20 tins army rations (8 oz. each)
   3 canteens (two 2-gal. and one 1-gal.) containing 5 gal-
       lons of water

                    total weight of food—45 lbs., 10 oz.
                    total weight of full canteens—57 lbs., 8 oz.

      Personal Flying Equipment (Orient Flight—1931)

   2 flying suits—electrically heated
   2 pr. flying boots (sheepskin lined)
   2 pr. heavy wool socks
   2 pr. light wool socks
   2 winter helmets
   2 summer helmets
   2 pr. goggles
   2 pr. mittens (wool lined)
     ear cotton
   2 life preservers (collapsible)
     personal clothing

      Personal Equipment (Orient Flight—1931)

     clothing and personal equipment 18 lbs. each
     total 36 lbs. including—
   2 blankets (used to wrap clothing and personal equip-
       ment)
   2 cotton ropes (to tie blanket bundles)
     passports, clearances, and certificates

Radio Equipment (Orient Flight—1931)

1 Pan American Airways standard plane radio transmit-
    ter with dynamotor and type A.C.C. receiver (15
    watt C.W. telegraph transmitter)
1 key assembly
1 pr. head-phones
1 trailing antenna assembly
    transmitting coils for following frequencies: 333, 500,
      3130, 5615, 8450, 13240 KC.
    receiving coils to cover the range of 17 to 150 meters,
      also the range of 600 to 1100 meters
    (The plane's storage battery was also used to operate
      the radio.)
1 direction finder (fixed loop type)
1 emergency radio transmitter and receiver complete for
    independent operation (encased in padded, water-
    tight box) (operated by dry cells), complete weight
    44 lbs.
1 repair box containing extra tubes, testing wire, extra
    antenna weight, tape, special antenna weight for
    emergency installation in flight, fuses, and miscel-
    laneous spares
1 extra antenna wire
1 hydrometer
    List of Fixed and Land Stations (cut down)
    Radio Aids to Navigation (cut down)
    pad, papers, pencils, clips, rubber bands
    flashlights (Listed under Navigation Equipment)

Navigation Equipment (Orient Flight—1931)

1 bubble sextant
2 chronometers
1 Weems Line of Position book
1 Nautical Almanac
1 slide rule
1 protractor
1 pr. dividers
    calculation forms, paper, pencils

charts and maps, both local and general, covering entire route

small globe of the world

1 battery flashlight (5-cell) with extra bulb

1 generator flashlight with extra bulb

Plane and Engine Equipment (Orient Flight—1931)

1 bilge pump

2 bilge-pump hoses

1 gasoline and oil funnel (aluminum)

2 gasoline felts

1 engine hand crank

1 iron anchor

1 sea anchor

1 canvas bag for emergency stone or sand anchor

1 anchor rope

2 wing ropes

1 anchor light

1 can tetraethyl lead

1 can light oil

1 can bitumastic paint

1 duralumin sheet (for emergency repairs)

1 bag duralumin rivets, bolts, nuts, washers, etc., for pontoon repairs

1 bag of magneto spare parts

1 extra pontoon cap

1 hatchet (to be used as hammer) (Listed under Emergency Equipment for Forced Landing on Land)

1 engine and accessory manual

1 tool bag

1 grease gun

1 cylinder stud wrench

1 cylinder stud-wrench handle

1 spark-plug wrench

1 spark-plug wrench handle

1 adjustable wrench—6"

1 intake manifold wrench

1 pr. pliers

1 cold chisel

1 carburetor jet wrench

1 valve-adjustment wrench
1 screwdriver—4"
1 coil safety wire
1 brace
  assortment of metal drills
1 file
  several hack-saw blades
2 magneto wrenches
1 file—3-corner
1 valve-clearance gauge
1 emery cloth
1 pontoon gas-tank measure
1 hydrometer (Listed under Radio Equipment)
3 spark plugs

The radio equipment carried in the *Sirius* consisted of the standard Pan American Airways model 10-C, 15 watt C.W. telegraph transmitter with dynamotor and type A.C.C. receiver. In addition to the regular plane radio, an emergency radio transmitting and receiving set was carried. This was inclosed in a water-tight, crash-proof box and was completely self-contained. It was designed for use on a rubber life raft in case of a forced landing at sea.

Both sets were constructed and installed under the supervision of Mr. Hugo Leuteritz, chief communication engineer of Pan American Airways, who also laid out the plans for radio communication during the flight.

Log of Flight to Orient—1931

July 27	20 : 00 G.M.T.	Took off Flushing Bay, New York.
	21 : 25 G.M.T.	Landed Washington, D.C.
July 28	17 : 30 G.M.T.	Took off Washington, D.C.
	19 : 25 G.M.T.	Landed Flushing Bay, New York.
July 29	17 : 50 G.M.T.	Took off Flushing Bay, New York.
	20 : 20 G.M.T.	Landed North Haven, Maine.

July 30	18 : 06 G.M.T.	Took off North Haven, Maine.
	21 : 36 G.M.T.	Landed Ottawa, Ontario.
August 1	14 : 50 G.M.T.	Took off Ottawa, Ontario.
	19 : 17 G.M.T.	Landed Moose Factory, Ontario.
August 2	16 : 00 G.M.T.	Took off Moose Factory, Ontario.
	23 : 50 G.M.T.	Landed Churchill, Manitoba.
August 3	18 : 47 G.M.T.	Took off Churchill, Manitoba.
	22 : 02 G.M.T.	Landed Baker Lake, Northwest Territories.
August 4	23 : 35 G.M.T.	Took off Baker Lake, Northwest Territories.
August 5	11 : 10 G.M.T.	Landed Aklavik, Northwest Territories.
August 8	03 : 42 G.M.T.	Took off Aklavik, Northwest Territories.
	10 : 07 G.M.T.	Landed Point Barrow, Alaska.
August 11	04 : 57 G.M.T.	Took off Point Barrow, Alaska.
	10 : 15 G.M.T.	Landed Shishmaref Inlet, Alaska.
	20 : 07 G.M.T.	Took off Shishmaref Inlet, Alaska.
	21 : 55 G.M.T.	Landed Safety Harbor, Nome, Alaska.
August 14	20 : 02 G.M.T.	Took off Safety Harbor, Nome, Alaska.
August 15	06 : 55 G.M.T.	Landed Karaginski Island, Kamchatka.
August 16	01 : 45 G.M.T.	Took off Karaginski Island, Kamchatka.
	06 : 02 G.M.T.	Landed Petropavlovsk, Kamchatka.
August 19	01 : 39 G.M.T.	Took off Petropavlovsk, Kamchatka.
	07 : 45 G.M.T.	Landed Ketoi Island, Chishima group.

August 21		Towed to Buroton Bay, Shimushiru Island, Chishima group.
August 22	05 : 14 G.M.T.	Took off Buroton Bay, Shimushiru Island, Chishima group.
	08 : 12 G.M.T.	Landed Shana, Etorofu Island, Chishima group.
August 23	05 : 23 G.M.T.	Took off Shana, Etorofu Island, Chishima group.
	08 : 05 G.M.T.	Landed Kunashiri Island, Chishima group.
	22 : 26 G.M.T.	Took off Kunashiri Island, Chishima group.
	22 : 54 G.M.T.	Landed Nemuro, Hokkaido, Japan.
August 25	23 : 22 G.M.T.	Took off Nemuro, Hokkaido, Japan.
August 26	05 : 10 G.M.T.	Landed Kasimigaura (Tokyo), Japan.
September 13	03 : 22 G.M.T.	Took off Kasimigaura, Japan.
	06 : 27 G.M.T.	Landed Osaka, Japan.
September 17	03 : 58 G.M.T.	Took off Osaka, Japan.
	07 : 01 G.M.T.	Landed Fukuoka, Japan.
September 18	23 : 56 G.M.T.	Took off Fukuoka, Japan.
September 19	06 : 10 G.M.T.	Landed Lotus Lake, Nanking, China.
September 20	to October 2	Various survey flights over the flooded areas of China.

After turning over in the Yangtze, the *Sirius* was carried to Shanghai on the deck of the British airplane carrier *Hermes*. From Shanghai it was shipped to the Lockheed Aircraft factory in California for repairs. In addition to the flight to the Orient and various flights in the United States, the *Sirius* made a thirty-thousand-mile survey flight around the North Atlantic Ocean in 1933. It is now in the American Museum of Natural History in New York City.